Debra Eason

ESSENTIALS
GCSE D&T
Textiles Technology

Contents

Contents

The Need for Textiles

Textiles

Textiles play an important part in our lives. They **contribute to** our **general well-being** and provide…
- **protection** from the elements, e.g. shelter and clothing
- **practical tools**
- **comfort**
- **decoration**.

There are many different kinds of textile products. The table contains just some examples.

'**Textiles**' is a general term used to describe **any product that is made from a fabric**. That fabric can be…
- knitted
- woven
- bonded or felted.

Function	Examples
Shelter	• Tents
Protection	• Underwear • Outdoor clothing • Accessories, e.g. hats, gloves and shoes
Comfort	• Interior products, e.g. curtains and bedding
Decoration	• One-off art and craft pieces, e.g. wall-hangings
Toys and games	• Soft toys
Practical tools	• Nappies • Tea towels • Sacks

Advanced Uses

Textiles also have **advanced applications** in a wide range of industries, including…
- roads and infrastructure
- civil engineering
- transport
- flooring
- medicine
- agriculture
- architecture
- specialised protective clothing.

Specialist Equipment and Tools

Lots of **specialist tools and equipment** are used to make textile products. They have **special features** that allow you to **carry out a specific task** correctly and effectively.

Tools and equipment can be divided into the following areas:
- **colour and design** equipment
- **pressing** equipment
- **sewing and joining** equipment
- **advanced** equipment
- **components** (i.e. items that become part of the final product).

This section looks at **tools and equipment** that are **commonly available in schools**. These items tend to be suited to **small-scale production** rather than mass-production.

Colour and Design Equipment

Batik pots are heat resistant pots that are used to **melt wax** for Batik (see p.56). Tools called **tjantings** are used to draw on fabrics with the hot wax.

Screen printing is one method of applying patterns to fabrics. A **screen with a special mesh** is placed over the fabric. A tool called a **squeegee** is then used to push the **pigment through the mesh** onto the fabric.

Fabric crayons and pens are dyes in **solid form** that can be used on both synthetic and natural fabrics. Ironing on the reverse of the fabric provides **heat**, which **'sets' the design**. It can then be hand washed safely at 40°C.

Batik Pot

Screen Printing Equipment

Pressing Equipment

Irons are used for **pressing** garments and also for **finishing** them, e.g. creating creases.

A **heat press** is a machine that can be used to **transfer printed designs** from specialist paper onto fabrics. It can also be used to pleat fabrics and create special effects.

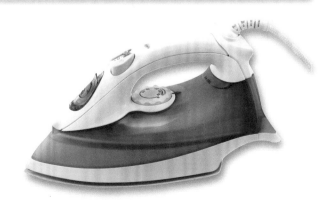

Equipment and Tools

Sewing Machines

There are different types of sewing machines that are suited to different tasks:

A standard sewing machine…
- is used to **join fabrics** and do **simple embroidery**
- has **limited features**.

An **embroidery machine**…
- is similar to a standard machine but with **additional features**
- can create lots of different **decorative stitches**.

A **computerised sewing machine**…
- is an **advanced sewing machine** with many features
- is controlled by a **computer interface**
- can produce designs that are digitised and sent to the machine by a computer.

An **overlocker**…
- is a specialised sewing machine used **for joining and finishing** fabrics
- gives seams and hems a **professional finish**
- can also be used for adding **decorative edgings** to fabrics.

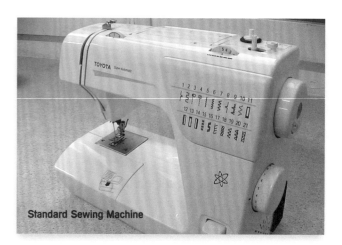

Standard Sewing Machine

Overlocker

Other Machines

Knitting machines are used to create fabrics, garments and textile products that are **patterned or textured**. They can be **linked to a computer** to speed up manufacture.

There are different types of **weaving looms** that are used to produce fabrics:
- hand looms
- ground looms
- backstrap looms
- frame looms.

Some can also be linked to computers.

NB: Many machines have fast-moving parts and needles – always check the settings and safeguards before use.

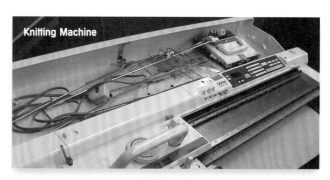

Knitting Machine

Weaving Loom

Non-Machine Based Equipment

Dressmaker's mannequins…
- are used to obtain the **correct size and fit** for a garment
- can be adjusted to different measurements and are available for all different shapes and sizes.

Scissors…
- come in many shapes and sizes
- each have a different purpose, e.g. pattern cutting and pinking.

Pinking shears have **serrated edges** for…
- finishing off the edges of fabric to **prevent fraying**
- producing **decorative edges**.

Tape measures…
- are used for measuring out patterns or garments
- can be curved easily, making them ideal for textiles.

Embroidery frames…
- are used to **hold fabrics in place**
- can be used for hand or machine embroidery.

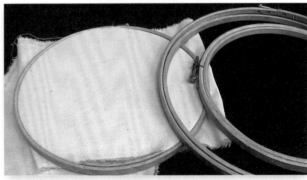

Quick Test

1. List three functions of textiles products.
2. Name two industries that use textiles for advanced applications.
3. What substance is melted in Batik pots?
4. What tool is used to push pigment through a mesh when screen printing?
5. Give one reason for using an overlocker.
6. What is the purpose of pinking shears?
7. What is a component?

KEY WORDS
Make sure you understand these words before moving on!
- Components
- Batik
- Screen printing
- Heat press
- Embroidery machine
- Overlocker
- Knitting machine
- Weaving loom
- Mannequin
- Pinking shears

Research

The Purpose of Research

Research involves…
- **collecting and collating** (gathering together) **information**
- **analysing and reporting** the **findings**.

Research helps identify…
- **factors** that affect **consumer choice**, e.g. cost, quality, style, etc.
- consumer **preferences within** certain **target markets**.

This information can be used to help you make decisions when designing and developing products.

There are two different types of research:
- **primary research**
- **secondary research**.

Primary Research

Primary research involves gathering the information **yourself**. Here are some common methods used:
- shows and exhibitions
- focus groups
- questionnaires / surveys.

Questionnaires and surveys are the most popular method of collecting and analysing consumer information. They can take the form of face-to-face, telephone or postal questionnaires, which…
- need a **large sample size** to produce reliable and helpful results
- can be **general**, e.g. target a random cross-section of society, or **specific**, e.g. target a specific consumer group
- require questions that are clear and **focused**
- should **avoid leading questions** and **use** lots of **closed questions** (which require people to choose from a number of set responses).

Questionnaire

NAME: ....

AGE: Under 20 ☐
      21 to 25 ☐
      26 to 30 ☐
      31 to 35 ☐
      35 Plus ☐

SEX: Male ☐
      Female ☐

1. Who do live with?
☐ Alone
☐ Parents
☐ Partner
☐ Partner and Children

2. Who makes the decisions on what to buy when shopping for new interior decor?
☐ Me
☐ My partner
☐ Its a Family decision
☐ My Interior Decorator

3. Do you buy Interior Decoration Magazines?
☐ Weekly
☐ Monthly
☐ Occasionally
☐ Never

4. Are you influenced by what you see in magazines?
☐ Yes
☐ Sometimes
☐ Occasionally
☐ Never

5. What type of colours do you prefer for furnishings?
☐ Bright
☐ Deep
☐ Neutral

6. How often do you change your interior decor?
☐ Every year
☐ Every other year
☐ When its necessary
☐ When I can afford it
☐ Never

7. Is price important to you?
☐ No
☐ Yes
☐ Sometimes

8. What is a consideration for you when buying interior decoration? (tick as many as applicable)
☐ Colour
☐ Texure
☐ Comfort
☐ Size
☐ Practicality
☐ Durability
☐ Child friendly
☐ Price
☐ Brand
☐ Current Trend
☐ Discount

Primary Research (Cont.)

Shows and exhibitions are a good place to **research new styles, trends and products** on the market.

Focus groups bring together a small **group of consumers**, so that designers can…

- ask questions about **how products are used** by consumers
- gain **feedback on designs** and prototypes in development
- **observe people** using existing products
- consider the **ergonomics** and **anthropometrics** of a product.

Secondary Research

Secondary research relies on information that has been **collected by other people**. Secondary sources include…

- statistics
- market reports
- websites
- trade publications, e.g. specialist magazines
- newspapers
- books.

Inspiration for Design

Designers can gain **inspiration** from many different places:

- **Art** – different forms of art, both classic and contemporary.
- **Graphics and photographs** – in books and magazines.
- **Materials and fabrics** – swatches of fabrics, wallpapers and colour samples.
- **Exhibitions, fairs and shows** – existing designs, both practical and avant-garde.
- **Cinema** – mainstream, art-house and world films, characters and animation.
- **Travel** – different cultures, traditions and lifestyles.
- **Architecture, furniture and interior design** – functional design that impacts on how we live.
- **Nature** – including landscapes, plants, flowers, animals and the ocean.

Research

Product Analysis

Product analysis involves **disassembling** (taking apart) an **existing product** to identify its key features.

The following process can help to develop a new product or improve an existing product:

Analyse...	Assess...	Identify...
<ul><li>the **function**</li><li>the **style**</li><li>key design **features**</li><li>the **construction** methods used</li><li>**fibre** types / content</li><li>whether any specialised fabrics have been used and what they are</li><li>whether the product has been made with **eco-design** and **environmental issues** in mind.</li></ul>	<ul><li>the **ergonomics** of the product</li><li>the size, using standard **anthropometric** measurements</li><li>how many **components**, parts or pattern pieces the product has</li><li>the possible **method of manufacture**</li><li>the **cost** of the product (compare this to other existing products)</li><li>whether it can be made with less components, parts or pieces.</li></ul>	<ul><li>any environmental issues associated with the product, e.g. method of applying colour, fibre used, recycling possibilities and life cycle of the product</li><li>the **colour application** method that was used</li><li>the methods of applying **embellishments** or patterns that have been used</li><li>any **trimmings** used in the product and where they're applied</li><li>all components used in the product</li><li>the **care label**, aftercare and product maintenance details</li><li>any **finishes** that have been applied to the product and how they affect it</li><li>any legal or **BSI standards** relating to the product</li><li>the method of **fabric construction**, e.g. whether it's knitted, woven, felted or non-woven</li><li>the **sizes** that the product is available in.</li></ul>

Industrial Practices

In industry, **designers** spend relatively little time on research in comparison to **developing ideas**.

They will then find out what consumers think of the new designs before manufacture, using surveys and focus groups.

Designers monitor high street fashion trends and carry out '**intelligence gathering**'. This is the process of gathering lots of detailed information about their target market.

Analysing and Evaluating

Following any research exercise, you need to **analyse and evaluate** the information gathered to establish...

- if there is a **clear trend** in the data (i.e. if a majority of the people surveyed agree on certain points)
- how it will **impact on the design**.

Research findings can be displayed using...

- **ICT**, e.g. tables, pie charts, star profiles, line graphs, histograms, pictographs
- a **mood board** (with notes) to provide a visual summary.

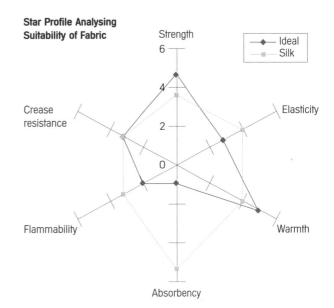

Quick Test

1. What are the two different categories of research?
2. What is disassembly of a product?
3. Give one reason for holding a focus group.
4. Name three possible sources of design inspiration.
5. Why is it important for have a large sample size for surveys?

KEY WORDS

Make sure you understand these words before moving on!

- Target market
- Primary research
- Secondary research
- Sample size
- Focus group
- Ergonomics
- Anthropometrics
- Disassembling
- Intelligence gathering

Specifications

Specifications

There are three types of **specification**:

Design Specification	Product Specification (see p.32)	Manufacturing Specification (see p.33)
• Created **from the design brief after research** has been carried out. • Sets out the **essential** and **desirable criteria** for the design.	• Drawn up once a **decision** has been made about which proposals **to develop further**. • **Identifies** the **materials** and **equipment** needed to make the product in the **prototype stage**.	• Produced **after** the product has undergone **final modifications**. • Provides **comprehensive** material and equipment **lists**. • **Identifies** all the **tasks** that need to be completed, **in sequence**, to manufacture the product.

Specification Considerations

The following elements need to be considered when producing a specification:

- **Form** – what shape should the product to be?
- **Function** – what does the product need to do?
- **User requirements** – what does the target market need / want?
- **Performance requirements** – what properties does the product need to do its job, e.g. strong, waterproof?
- **Materials and components** – what will the product be made from?
- **Scale of production** – how many do you need to produce?
- **Budget** – how much money is available for materials and production?
- **Sustainability** – how can the product's impact on the environment be reduced?

Design Specification

Your design specification will normally…
- be a list of **bullet points**
- provide **guidelines** to help you **focus your design ideas**
- include all the **key points from the brief**
- take into account the **findings of your research**
- list all the **essential criteria** you must include in your designs
- include **desirable criteria** you would like to include in your designs if possible.

Colour

Colour is the effect of different **light waves** being **reflected and absorbed** by a material.

Colour plays an important part in textiles and fashion design.

Colours are divided into...

- **primary colours** (red, yellow and blue) – can't be mixed from any other colours
- **secondary colours** (orange, green and purple) – mixed from **two** primary colours
- **tertiary colours** – mixed from **three** primary colours.

A colour wheel can be a simple representation of the primary and secondary colours, but most designers will use a version that includes tertiary colours.

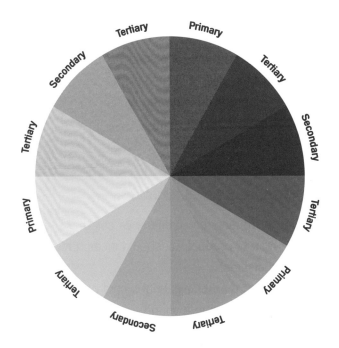

Describing Colour

Colours can be further described using the following terms:

- **Monochromatic** – the use of shades, tones and tints of just one colour, e.g. black, including greys through to white.
- **Complementary (or contrasting) colours** – colours on **opposite sides of the colour wheel** which produce a strong contrast, e.g. red and green.
- **Harmonious colours** – colours that **work well** (harmoniously) together, e.g. yellow and green.
- **Warm colours** – give a sense of warmth, e.g. reds and yellows (think 'fire').
- **Cold colours** – give a sense of coolness, e.g. blues (think 'water').

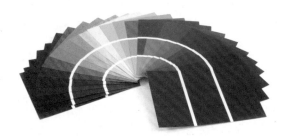

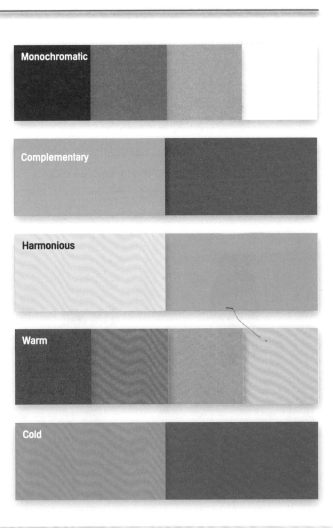

Colour and Design

Describing Colour (Cont.)

- **Hue** – the **actual colour** that you see, e.g. crimson or royal blue.
- **Shade** – the **depth of colour**; usually refers to a hue that has been darkened by mixing it with black.
- **Tint** – produced by **adding white** to a colour.
- **Tone** – how **light or dark** the hue is (on a scale of tints and shades).

Red Hue	Yellow Hue	Purple Hue

Darker shade — Lighter tint	Darker shade — Lighter tint	Darker shade — Lighter tint
Tone	Tone	Tone

Colour Considerations

The following factors will **influence** colour choice:
- the **type of product**, i.e. should it catch the eye or be discreet?
- the **target market**, e.g. bright, bold colours might be better suited to a young age-group.

Other things to remember when selecting a colour palette include...
- colours can have different effects against different **skin tones**, e.g. some warm colours work well with dark skin but not pale skin
- colours have different **symbolic** meanings for different religions and cultures, e.g. red represents prosperity in China
- colours appear different depending on the **intensity and type of light**, e.g. bright colours look more intense in direct sunlight.

Pattern and Texture

Patterns can be **regular** (i.e. repeating) **or irregular**.

It's important to think about scale:

- Large and small patterns can create **different effects**, e.g. small patterns can look 'busy'.
- The design may need to work on **different scales**, e.g. on a pillowcase and a duvet cover.

Texture can add 'interest' to a fabric. It will also affect its **handle and feel**. This means it's important to think about texture in the context of how the product will be used, e.g. a rough, itchy fabric would not be suitable for baby clothes.

Line and Style

Lines can be used to create **visual effects.**
For example…

- vertical lines will make things look tall and narrow
- horizontal lines make things look short and wide
- diagonal lines can have a very dramatic effect.

Style refers to the **overall effect** created by a combination of elements like shape, colour, line, pattern, and texture.

Different styles are associated with different periods in time, e.g. monochromatic prints and A-line shapes are typical of one style from the 1960s.

Many designers develop their own distinctive style, which is instantly recognisable, e.g. Vivienne Westwood.

Quick Test

1. When mixing colour, what is the difference between a tint and a shade?
2. What is a monochromatic colour scheme?
3. What are complementary colours?
4. What does a design specification set out?
5. At what stage should a manufacturing specification be produced?

KEY WORDS
Make sure you understand these words before moving on!

- Specification
- Primary colour
- Secondary colour
- Tertiary colour
- Monochromatic
- Complementary
- Harmonious
- Hue
- Shade
- Tint
- Tone
- Style

Practice Questions

1 Complete the following sentence.

'Textiles' is a general term used to describe...

....

2 Give two examples of pieces of equipment used for...

a) colour and design.

i) .... **ii)** ....

b) pressing.

i) .... **ii)** ....

c) sewing and joining.

i) .... **ii)** ....

3 Name three types of machine used in the production of textiles, which can be linked to a computer and used to produce digitised designs.

a) .... **b)** ....

c) ....

4 Name three methods of gathering information for primary research.

a) .... **b)** ....

c) ....

5 Briefly explain the difference between primary and secondary research.

....

....

6 Use the words provided to fill in the gaps and complete the following sentences.

new	**existing**	**identify**	**disassembly**

.... is the process of taking an existing product apart to ....

its key features and how it has been made. The information gained through this process can help you to

develop a .... product or improve an .... product.

7 Which of the following statements about product specifications are true? Tick the correct options.

    A It lists all the materials required. ◯

    B It includes a 'wish list' of desirable criteria. ◯

    C It lists all the tools and equipment required. ◯

    D It is produced at the very start of a design project from the design brief. ◯

    E It is produced after all the final modifications have been made to the prototype. ◯

    F It identifies all the tasks that need to be completed in sequence. ◯

    G It provides comprehensive instructions on how to make the prototype. ◯

8 Draw a line to match each type of colour to the correct description.

Primary	Mixed from three primary colours in different amounts.
Secondary	Can't be mixed from any other colours.
Tertiary	Mixed from two primary colours.

9 What is a harmonious colour palette? Tick the correct option.

    A A palette that features different tints and shades of a single colour. ◯

    B A palette made up of contrasting colours. ◯

    C A palette made up of colours that work well together. ◯

    D A palette that features a balance of warm and cold colours. ◯

10 Write down the name of a textiles product that needs to have…

    a) bright, eye-catching colours.

    b) colours that help the product blend into the background.

    c) a soft texture.

Textiles and the Environment

The Impact of Textiles on the Environment

Textile products have a **large impact** on the **environment**. This is because at every stage of the product's life cycle...

- **energy** and **resources** are used
- waste is produced.

Due to the amount of energy needed to make and care for textile products, they often have a large **carbon footprint**. A carbon footprint is a measure of the amount of carbon dioxide produced directly or indirectly by an individual or product.

Manufacturing Textiles

Dyeing and finishing **processes use lots of chemicals**. For example...

- chemical dyes
- resins to make fabrics shrink proof
- softeners to improve the feel of the fabric.

In addition to producing lots of chemical waste they...

- **require energy** to drive the machinery
- **use and contaminate** large volumes of **water**.

Possible solutions for reducing these problems include...

- using **cold water dyes** or dyes that require **less energy** in processing
- using renewable sources of energy, e.g. wind turbines and solar energy

- reducing the need for very dark dyes, which require a large amount of rinsing to remove excess dye
- using **natural dyes** from plants and insects
- using **naturally coloured yarns**, such as cotton, to eliminate the dye process completely
- trying to develop finishing processes that require less energy
- using **fabrics** that **already have** the **properties** needed, e.g. lyocell is resistant to shrinkage and wrinkling
- using biomass (organic waste) to produce biofuels for transportation.

Sustainability

Natural fibres and dyes need to come from **sustainable** sources, i.e. sources that are carefully **managed** so that plants and animals are **replaced**. Collecting large amounts from the wild would reduce natural reserves and, in some cases, could lead to extinction.

Scientists are exploring the possibility of producing natural materials without the use of plants and animals. For example, 'victimless leather' is 'grown' from cells in a laboratory. This is called **biotechnology**.

Laundry and Aftercare   AQA • OCR

Most textile products **need cleaning and maintaining** throughout their life. This is done through processes like washing, dry-cleaning and ironing.

Energy used in these processes can be reduced by...

- creating fabrics and clothing that are **durable** and **easy to care for** and repair (i.e. have a longer life span)

- providing more **information** to the consumer to enable them to **care for the product effectively**
- producing clothes and textiles products that can be **washed** at **low temperatures** or in cold water
- **avoiding** fabrics or products that are dry-clean only
- using fabrics that require little or **no ironing**.

Textiles and the Environment

Waste Textiles

Off-cuts and other textiles often go to waste. Possible methods of **reusing** and **reducing** this **waste** are…

- to use **computerised lay planning** and pattern cutting to reduce the waste
- to use **fabric scraps** within the **automotive industry** or to produce products such as emergency relief blankets
- to look at ways of using waste textiles in the manufacture of new textile products, for example, Muji has a range of textile products made from textile waste and excess yarns that would normally be thrown away.

Design Obsolescence Edexcel • OCR

The **fashion industry** encourages consumers to **continuously update** their wardrobes with the **latest trends**, even though their old clothes are still in good condition. This leads to goods becoming obsolete. It is called '**design obsolescence**' (or planned obsolescence) and it generates a vast amount of potential waste.

Disposal

The way in which a product is **disposed** of at the end of its **life cycle** is **critical**.

If a product is thrown out as **refuse**, it will be put in a **landfill site** or **incinerated**.

The following methods of disposal **prevent materials from being wasted** and **save energy** (as fewer new products and materials need to be manufactured):

- **Reuse** the product, e.g. sell on through a charity shop
- **Recycle** the materials, e.g. use the materials to make another product.

Quick Test

1. Why do textile products have such a large impact on the environment?
2. Name two manufacturing processes that use chemicals.
3. Why is it not sustainable to throw textile products out as refuse?
4. Give one reason why textile products continue to have an impact on the environment after purchase.
5. What is the main problem caused by design obsolescence?

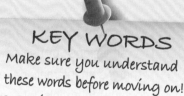

KEY WORDS

Make sure you understand these words before moving on!

- Environment
- Carbon footprint
- Design Obsolescence
- Recycle

Designer Responsibility

Factors	Ways of Reducing Impact	Example
Design	• Design products for **durability**, **comfort** and **function** (as opposed to fashion). • Design products that are **reusable** rather than disposable. • Try to source local materials to cut down on transportation.	
Fabrics	• **Consider** the specification of the **fabric**, e.g. think about using organic rather than inorganic cotton. • Consider the specification of the **colours** (this will determine the dyeing, printing and finishing processes used). • **Avoid** using fabrics that need **dry cleaning or special care**. • Consider using **recycled** materials.	
Components	• Check **what components are made from** and how they're produced (many buttons are made from plastics and zips and buckles are electroplated to prevent rust, which produces a toxic sludge). • Is it possible to **reduce** the number of **components** used? • Consider using **recycled** components.	
Production	• Consider the use of **reusable pattern blocks**. • Review how to **minimise fabric and yarn wastage**. • Use processes that create less waste. • Explore methods of reducing greenhouse gas emissions* or use carbon offsetting. *There is an international agreement between industrial countries to do this. It is called the Kyoto Protocol.	
End Use	• Provide **clear aftercare instructions**. • Include labels that give **information** about **how to recycle** the materials. • Donate or re-sell items that are no longer needed to charity shops or organisations in need.	

Recycling

The following symbol is used to show that a product or material can be recycled. It is called the Mobius Loop.

To **recycle** a product or material **means to reuse** it. It may need some processing or treatment before it can be reused.

There are three main types of recycling:
- **Primary recycling** – the textile product can be **reused in its current state**, e.g. by taking old clothes to charity shops or clothing banks.
- **Physical or secondary recycling** – the product is **torn, shredded, melted or ground** before being reused, e.g. old woollen garments can be shredded and reused as stuffing in bedding or industrial felting.
- Chemical or **tertiary recycling** – products can be **broken down and reformulated**, e.g. PET plastic bottles can be broken down into fibres and then spun into polyester to make fleeces and duvets.

The Importance of Recycling

Textiles products use a lot of **natural resources**, e.g. cotton, linen and silk, so it is **important to reuse** them rather than let them go to waste.

The key reasons for recycling are to…
- **save energy**
- **save raw materials**
- **reduce the need** to manufacture new products (recycling often uses less energy).

Nowadays designers often try to think of new ways to recycle products.

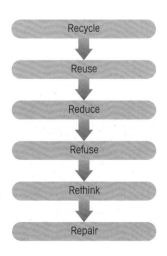

Recycle → Reuse → Reduce → Refuse → Rethink → Repair

Recycling and Ethical Goods

The 6 'R's of Recycling | OCR

R	Method
Recycle	• Recycle materials that can be recycled. • Buy products made from recycled materials. • Disassemble old products and reuse the materials in new ones.
Reuse	• Buy / design products that can be reused (for the same / different purpose). • Reuse products by adapting them for a new use.
Reduce	• Reduce the amount of materials used and wasted. • Reduce the amount of energy used and waste produced by production processes. • Reduce obsolescence. • Reduce the carbon footprint of a product.
Refuse	• Refuse to buy / design products that are not sustainable / recyclable.
Rethink	• Think about how you can approach design issues differently. • Think about how you can reuse a product or its materials rather than let it go to waste.
Repair	• Repair products rather than buying new ones.

Ethical Goods
AQA • OCR

The **choices** you make when buying goods on the high street or Internet have a direct **impact on others**.

As long as people continue to buy cheap products that are produced in factories with poor conditions and pay for workers, these factories will continue to operate.

As a **designer**, when sourcing **fabrics and components** you need to be aware of...
• **where** they came from
• **how** they were produced.

As a **consumer** you can look for **labels** that identify products as being safer for the environment and / or fairly produced. These goods might not be the cheapest, but the labels **provide assurance** that they have been **produced ethically**.

The Ethical Trading Initiative (ETI) is a group of companies, charities and organisations that was founded in 1998 to work towards improving conditions in global supply chains.

Ethical Goods (Cont.) AQA • OCR

FSC (Forestry Stewardship Council)	Applies to **wood** and wood products (e.g. paper fibres) that are independently certified to assure customers that they come from forests that are **managed** to meet the social, economic and ecological needs of present and future generations.	FSC
European Eco Label	Applies to **products and services** where steps have been taken to **minimise** the **environmental impact** of their **whole life cycle** ('cradle to grave').	
The European Energy Label	Applies to **appliances**, e.g. freezers and washing machines, showing their level of **energy consumption** (where A or AA are the most efficient).	Energy / Washing machine / Manufacturer Model / Hotpoint WMA60 / More efficient / A / B / A
Confidence in Textiles / The Oeko-Tex® Label	Applies to **fabrics** that have been tested against the Oeko-Tex® Standard 100 to ensure they are **free from harmful substances**.	CONFIDENCE IN TEXTILES / Tested for harmful substances / according to Oeko-Tex Standard 100 / No. 00000000 Institut
FAIRTRADE Mark	Fairtrade provides a better deal for producers in **developing countries**. The FAIRTRADE Mark gives a guarantee to consumers that the farmers and workers have been paid a **fair and stable price** which covers the cost of **sustainable production**.	FAIRTRADE / Choose products with this Mark / www.fairtrade.org.uk
Mobius Loop	This label indicates **how much** (%) of the product is **made from recycled material** (this could be a mix of both virgin and recycled material).	35
Recyclable Plastic	This label identifies **the type of recyclable plastic used** (this example represents PET).	1

Quick Test

1. What can old woollen garments be recycled as?
2. Name two places you can take your old clothes to be recycled?
3. What can PET bottles be recycled into?
4. What does FSC stand for?
5. With 'Confidence in Textiles' what have the fabrics been tested for?
6. How many arrows does the Mobius Loop have?

KEY WORDS

Make sure you understand these words before moving on!
- Durability
- Aftercare
- Primary recycling
- Secondary recycling
- Tertiary recycling
- Reformulated
- Ethically
- Fairtrade
- Mobius Loop

Practice Questions

1 Choose the correct words from the options given to complete the following sentences.

aftercare   waste   resources   small   manufacturing   energy   large

Textile products have a .... impact on the environment. This is because many of

the .... processes and methods of .... produce

.... and use .... and ....

2 Briefly describe one way in which chemicals are used to enhance the properties of the fabric at the finishing stage.

....

3 Some fabrics made from mixed fibres need to by dyed twice, because the different fibres require different types of dye. Briefly explain why this is a problem for the environment.

....

....

....

4 Suggest two ways in which the dyeing process can be made more environmentally friendly.

a) ....

b) ....

5 Suggest two ways in which fabric scraps and off-cuts can be made use of to reduce textiles waste.

a) ....

b) ....

6 What is 'design obsolescence'?

....

....

7 What does FSC stand for? Tick the correct option.

A Fabric Sustainability Council   ◯   **B** Fibre Standards Committee   ◯

C Forestry Stewardship Commission   ◯   **D** Friendly, Sustainable Cotton   ◯

8 Which of the following statements are examples of responsible design? Tick the correct options.

A   Use delicate fabrics that require specialist cleaning. ⬭

B   Use organic, natural fibres from sustainable sources. ⬭

C   Take advantage of a fabric's natural properties so less processing is required. ⬭

D   Try to use as many components as possible. ⬭

E   Always use disposable patterns. ⬭

F   Include information on how to recycle the materials on the label. ⬭

G   Try to use naturally coloured yarns. ⬭

9 Draw lines between the boxes to match the different types of recycling to the correct description.

Primary recycling		Also called physical recycling; the materials are shredded or melted before being reused.
Secondary recycling		Also called chemical recycling; the materials are broken down and reformulated.
Tertiary recycling		The product is reusable in its existing state.

10 Suggest three ways in which you can recycle textile products at home.

a) ....

b) ....

c) ....

11 Which of the following statements about Fairtrade products are true? Tick the correct options ⬭

A   Fairtrade products are usually produced in developing countries. ⬭

B   Fairtrade products are produced in the UK. ⬭

C   The workers who produce Fairtrade products work in terrible conditions. ⬭

D   The suppliers of Fairtrade products are paid a fair price. ⬭

E   The Fairtrade label assures that the products are ethically produced. ⬭

F   Fairtrade products may be more expensive than similar products that don't carry the label. ⬭

Sketchbooks and Mood Boards

Using Sketchbooks AQA

Sketchbooks are great for designers because they can be taken anywhere. They can be used to **record ideas** as they occur and to **collect related information**. This might include…

- fabric samples
- trimmings
- drawings
- quick sketches
- paintings
- photographs
- notes / annotations
- possible colourways
- magazine / newspaper clippings.

Mood Boards AQA • OCR

Mood boards are a popular tool for commercial designers.

They help the designer to **communicate** the overall **style or 'feel'** they want to capture in their design.

A mood board…

- brings together a range of inspirational images, textures, patterns and colours
- provides a **visual summary** of the **overall theme or 'mood'** of the design
- doesn't contain detailed information about the end product
- should feature the main focal point just off-centre to draw the eye inwards.

Using Mood Boards AQA • OCR

Mood boards can be used…

- to provide a **focus** when developing new design ideas
- to **finalise** a palette of colours, textures and patterns
- to **develop** styles for garments and products
- in **surveys** to determine client or target market **requirements**
- to **communicate** ideas to clients.

Trend Forecasting

AQA • OCR

Trend boards…
- look similar to mood boards
- focus on **future trends** rather than current trends
- are usually created for a specific event, such as an exhibition.

Trend books…
- also focus on **future trends**
- are compilations of **data and images**
- are referred to time and time again throughout the development of a new product for the **visual inspiration** they provide.

Designers often **start work** on products and garments **two or more years before** they will be **in the shops**.

To ensure their products will be 'on trend', they rely on **special agencies** who **forecast future trends**.

These companies collect a lot of **information and data** about…
- **lifestyle**
- **popular culture**, e.g. films and music
- new **fibres** and **materials**
- **technological developments**
- what is happening in **other fields of design**.

They use this information to **predict** what the market will want and what colours, materials, shapes and **styles** will be in fashion in two or three year's time.

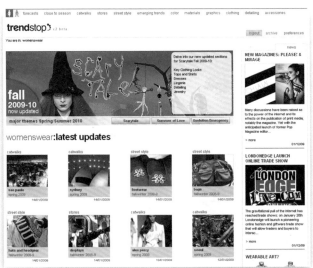

www.trendstop.com

Quick Test

1. A mood board provides detailed information about the final design of a product. **True** or **false**?
2. Do trend boards and trend books feature current trends or future trends?
3. List three areas that special agencies look at to help forecast trends.
4. Why is it important for designers to have information about possible future trends?

KEY WORDS
Make sure you understand these words before moving on!
- Mood board
- Target market
- Trend board
- Trend book
- Popular culture

Designing

Initial Ideas

Generating the initial ideas for a design is a creative process, but it's important not to get carried away.

It doesn't matter how exciting and innovative a design is, if it doesn't meet the criteria on the design specification, the design will be disregarded.

To make sure they stay focused, good designers constantly **refer to** their…

- **research** results
- **design specification**
- **mood board**.

Initial ideas tend to be captured using quick sketches.

Exploring Ideas

It is important to **explore** different **ideas** and **experiment** with **different techniques** at an early stage.

This will allow you to **select** the most **appropriate and effective ideas and techniques** when you start to develop and refine your designs for the final product.

Try experimenting with…

- colour
- texture
- proportion
- construction
- fabrics
- surface decoration
- embellishment
- ICT.

Colour

Explore…

- alternative **colour schemes**
- different methods of **applying colour**, e.g. fabric crayons, transfer crayons, printing and stencilling
- **layering colour** by combining techniques, e.g. tie-dye and fabric painting.

Tie-dye

Fabric Crayons

Texture

In textiles, 'texture' generally refers to the **tactile nature** (feel) of the fabric, but some prints and patterns give the appearance of texture too.

Ideas for textural designs can be explored by…
- looking at **nature**, e.g. plants, flowers, rocks and sea life
- experimenting with **yarn wrappings**
- combining different **textured fabrics**
- combining different textured ribbons and **trimmings**, e.g. to create embroidered borders
- using **techniques such as rubbings** (taken using transfer crayons on paper) which can then be transferred to fabric
- manipulating **fabrics** using dry heat, steam or stitching.

Proportion   OCR

Experiment with…
- the **size / scale** of the design
- the **relative proportions** of different elements within the design.

It is important that a product '**does its job**' and is **easy to use**. This means that when you make decisions about size and proportion, you need to consider…
- anthropometric data, i.e. average human measurements
- ergonomics, i.e. how people will use the product and what design features will help them to do this.

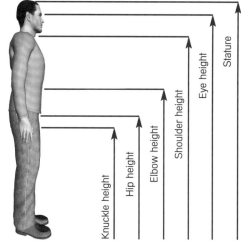

Average Measurements

Knuckle height, Hip height, Elbow height, Shoulder height, Eye height, Stature

Construction

To explore different construction methods, you could…
- **model garments** and products at 50% ($\frac{1}{2}$ scale) or 20% ($\frac{1}{5}$ scale) scale
- **practise** different skills and techniques on off-cuts of fabrics.

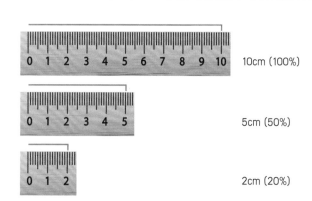

10cm (100%)

5cm (50%)

2cm (20%)

Designing

Fabrics

Experimenting with different **fabrics** will help you to **understand their properties**, so that you can…

- **select the most suitable** fabric for a job
- **combine** different fabrics in an innovative way.

You might try…

- stitching woollen and cotton fabrics together in a geometrical design, then machine washing on a hot setting – the wool will shrink and the cotton will remain the same size, creating an unusual effect
- dyeing fabrics, e.g. 100% cotton, 100% polyester and a 70/30% polycotton blend to compare results.

Surface Decoration

Surface decoration involves adding colour or texture to a fabric and can add **another dimension** to a design. You should explore various techniques like…

- **transfer printing** computer-generated designs onto fabrics
- other **printing** techniques
- **layering** prints, i.e. printing designs on top of each other
- **Batik, stencilling and painting**.

Embellishment

Embellishment is the addition of decorative components to **enhance** a design, but be careful not to over-use them. You could try…

- hand / machine **embroidery** techniques
- **laminating** fabrics and then embroidering them
- adding sequins, beads or ribbons.

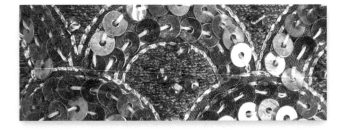

Using ICT

Try using a **computer** to…

- **develop patterns**
- **change the scale** of a design
- **create different texts** for embroidery using a font feature (e.g. Word Art)
- **manipulate digital images**.

Development

Development involves refining an idea to make it better, or to make the product easier to use. It should be done in the following sequence:

1 Initial Sketches

Quick sketches of ideas showing key details or outlines.

2 Detailed Drawings

Take a few initial sketches and make more detailed drawings. This is when you need to start thinking about colour, texture, proportion, etc. Refer to your research and design specification to ensure that all your choices are appropriate for the end product.

For fashion design, it's a good idea to have a few sample poses that you're happy with, and whenever you need to develop a garment you can quickly trace over a pose.

3 Further Refinement of Ideas

Take just one or two detailed drawings and refine them further – adapt and modify them until you're happy with all the elements of the design and it meets the criteria on your specification.

Modifications might include altering necklines, adding sleeves, adjusting dimensions, or changing the colour and size of a motif. You must be able to justify why you have…
- rejected / refined a particular idea
- changed colours, fabrics, methods, etc.

At this stage you should also produce some modelling samples of the techniques and methods you have decided on.

4 Final Images

Select the design you will use for the final product and produce final images showing the front, back and (where necessary) side views. These images must be in proportion / to scale. Use annotations or additional images to identify the key features of the design.

Quick Test

1 Suggest two different ways of applying colour to fabric.
2 What word is used to refer to the tactile nature of fabrics?
3 Suggest one method of practising construction techniques without producing the entire product.
4 Why is it essential to have a good understanding of the properties of different fabrics?
5 Which views of the product should final images include?

KEY WORDS

Make sure you understand these words before moving on!
- Proportion
- Construction
- Embellishment
- Texture
- Manipulating
- Anthropometric data
- Ergonomics
- Development
- Modifications

Product Specification

Copyright of Designs

In the textile and fashion industries, designs are sometimes copied. Copyright, patents and registered designs are just some ways in which a designer is protected. Relevant Acts of Parliament include…

- Copyright Designs and Patents Act, 1988
- Trade Marks Act, 1994.

The Product Specification

The **product specification** contains all the **instructions and information** needed **to produce a prototype** of the product. It needs to be very clear. Ask yourself – could someone else follow the instructions and make the prototype if they wanted to?

The product specification is also used to **calculate** the final **cost** of the product, so the information must be accurate.

A product specification contains the following:

1 A **working drawing** of the product – a black and white technical drawing that shows the…

- front and back views
- measurement details
- exploded drawings, highlighting key details where necessary
- details of seams, etc.

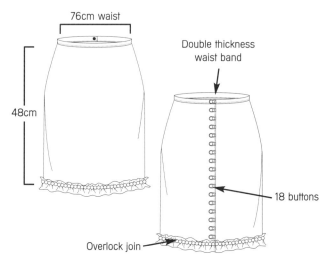

2 A **written description** of the finished product, including…

- a list of all components and fabrics
- quantities / amounts needed.

3 **Samples** of fabrics, colours, components, etc.

4 **Sizing details** of all the different elements of the design.

5 Appropriate **user instructions** and **aftercare information**.

Industry Specifications

In industry, the product and manufacturing specifications incorporate a…

- **fabric specification** – e.g. type, weight, colour fastness, finishes, abrasion resistance, feel / texture
- **garment specification** – style, size, dimensions, colours, type of fabrics
- **component specification** – fusings, interlinings, zips, fastenings.

Fabric Specification Sheet

Roller Blind Fabric

Diffuse Light	Moist Conditions	Flame Retardant	Computer Environments

Fabric Width:	250cm
Roll Length:	30m
Fabric Composition:	30% Polyester, 70% Vinyl on Polyester
Fabric Weight:	410g/m²
Fire Retardant:	BS 5867: 1980 Part 2 Type B
Openess Factor:	3%
UV Blockage:	Approximately 95%
Care and Washing:	Do not soak. Clean by gently wiping with a sponge.
Properties:	Recommended for moist conditions Flame retardant Diffuse Recommended for computer environments

Manufacturing Specification

The Manufacturing Specification

The **manufacturing specification** is produced **after the prototype** has been made and **incorporates** any final adjustments or **modifications**.

It provides a **detailed set of guidelines**, including written instructions, diagrams and flow charts, that should enable the **manufacturer** to **make the product** exactly as the designer envisaged.

A typical manufacturing specification might include…
- a list of materials and components
- a list of tools and equipment
- a detailed plan of work as a flow chart
- set time lines and guides for each stage of manufacture
- appropriate quality control checks
- details of the critical points in the making process
- a list of possible problems and solutions
- correct pattern annotation.

Quick Test

1. At what stage is the production specification produced?
2. List three things that a manufacturing specification should include.
3. Why is it important for a manufacturing specification to be clear and accurate?

KEY WORDS
Make sure you understand these words before moving on!
- Product specification
- Manufacturing specification

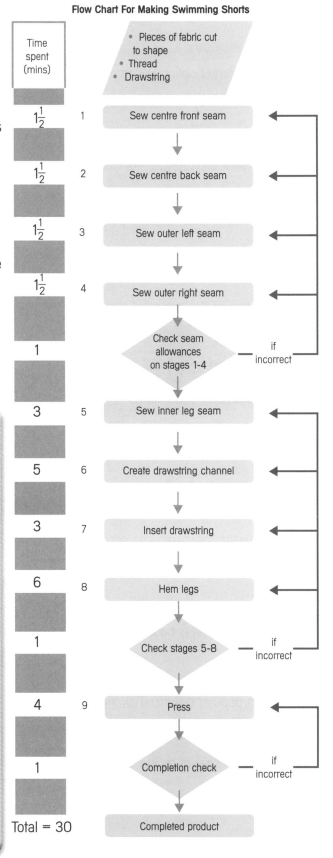

Flow Chart For Making Swimming Shorts

Practice Questions

1 Suggest two uses for a sketchbook.

a) ....

b) ....

2 Tick the correct option to complete the following sentence.

A manufacturing specification is produced…

    A   before making a prototype.   ⬭   **B**   after creating your initial ideas. ⬭

    C   after a prototype has been produced. ⬭   **D**   whilst producing the prototype. ⬭

3 Briefly explain what trend boards are.

....

....

4 Which two scales are most commonly used when modelling ideas? Tick the correct options.

    A   1:100 ⬭   **B**   1:5 ⬭

    C   1:500 ⬭   **D**   1:2 ⬭

5 What is an embellishment?

....

....

6 Write **anthropometric** or **ergonomic** alongside the following descriptions as appropriate.

  a)   A design that takes into account how the end-user will handle and use the product, making it easier for them to do so.

    ....

  b)   A design that is based on average human measurements to ensure it is an appropriate size.

    ....

7 What is popular culture? Tick the correct option.

    A   Museums and art galleries ⬭   **B**   Historical traditions ⬭

    C   Mainstream music, films, tv, etc. ⬭   **D**   Opera, ballet, theatre, etc. ⬭

8 Draw lines between the boxes to match the different terms to the correct description.

Proportion	It contains all the instructions and information needed to produce a prototype of the product.
Development	Experimenting with the size / scale of the design or different elements within the design.
Product specification	Involves refining an idea to make it better, or to make the product easier to use.

9 List four things that a working drawing needs to include.

a) ....

b) ....

c) ....

d) ....

10 What is the technique called when you transfer a raised image or pattern from an object onto paper using crayons? Tick the correct option.

A Scanning ◯   **B** Rubbing ◯

C Copying ◯   **D** Reassignment ◯

11 Which of the following statements about mood boards are true? Tick the correct options.

A It contains all the instructions and information needed to produce a prototype. ◯

B It provides a visual summary of the overall theme or 'mood' of the design. ◯

C It focuses on future trends for fashion. ◯

D It doesn't contain detailed information about the end product. ◯

E It brings together a range of inspirational images, textures, patterns and colours. ◯

12 In textile fabrics, what does the word texture generally refer to?

....

Fibres and Yarns

Fibres

All fabrics are made from tiny hair-like structures called **fibres**. They are either...
- **staple** (short) fibres
- **filament** (long) fibres.

There are three main groups of fibres:

Natural fibres come from...
- **animals**, e.g. wool, silk, alpaca, angora, camel hair, cashmere, mohair and vicuna
- **plants**, e.g. cotton, linen, jute, hemp and ramie.

Synthetic fibres are **man-made** from the by-products of oil. They include elastomeric, acrylic, aramid, modacrylic, polyamide, polyethylene, polyvinyl chloride (PVC). **Microfibres** are extremely **fine synthetic fibres**, e.g. polyester, nylon and Tactel®.

Regenerated fibres are made from a combination of **chemicals and cellulose waste**, e.g. viscose, lyocell, acetate, cupro, modal, tencel.

Cotton Fibres

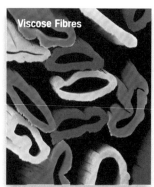
Viscose Fibres

Cotton Field

Yarns

Individual **fibres** are **weak**, but when they're made into **yarns** they take on **different properties**.

Yarns are made by **spinning and twisting fibres** together:
- The **worsted** spinning system produces a **smooth yarn**.
- The **woollen** spinning system produces a more **hairy yarn**.

Fibres can be **spun** in one of two ways:
- **S twist** (anticlockwise)
- **Z twist** (clockwise).

More **complex yarns** combine **equal** amounts of **S twists** and **Z twists** to **prevent distortion**.

The **long lengths** of yarn are wound onto **spools or cones**.

The **different types** of yarns are...
- spun yarns
- multi-filament yarns
- monofilament yarns
- assembled yarns
- folded yarns
- plied yarns
- complex yarns
- fancy yarns.

Bulk yarns are heavier and chunkier and are often used to make hats, scarves and sweaters.

Knitted Fabrics

Knitted fabrics are made from **yarn** in a series of **interlocking loops**.

Due to the loops, knitted fabrics are **elastic** (stretchy). **Further elasticity** can be added by using **elastane**, e.g. Lycra®.

Knitted fabrics are **warm**. This property can be **improved** by a finishing process called **napping** or **brushing**, which gives the fabric a fluffy surface, as used in fleeces.

Weft knitted fabrics...
- have **horizontal** (left to right) rows of knitted yarn
- have **horizontal ribs** on the wrong side
- have **V-shaped loops** on the face (right side)
- have **interlocking loops** above and below each row, which hold the fabric together
- include machine knitted fabrics like polyester fleece fabrics, **single jersey** (e.g. t-shirts), **double jersey** (e.g. sports shirts).

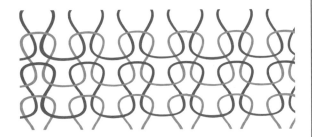

Warp knitted fabrics...
- have **interlocking loops** or chains that run **vertically** (up and down) down the fabric
- can only be **machine made**
- are **less elastic** and tend to be **firmer** fabric than weft knitted fabrics – they keep their shape well and don't usually ladder when cut
- include **lightweight** fabrics, like **nets** and **lace**, and **heavy** fabrics, like **terry toweling** and **velour**.

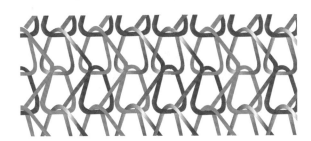

Woven Fabrics

Woven fabrics are constructed from **interlocking threads** or yarns. They're produced on a **weaving loom**.

Woven fabrics are made up of...
- **weft yarns**, which run **horizontally**
- **warp yarns**, which run **vertically**.

Woven fabrics...
- **fray easily** when cut
- are **strongest along the straight grain** of the fabric
- **lack elasticity**, although elastane can be added to give a bit more stretch
- are **stronger and firmer the closer the weave** is.

Due to the way it is constructed, a woven fabric has a...
- **selvedge** – an edge that won't fray
- **bias** – a diagonal or cross grain.

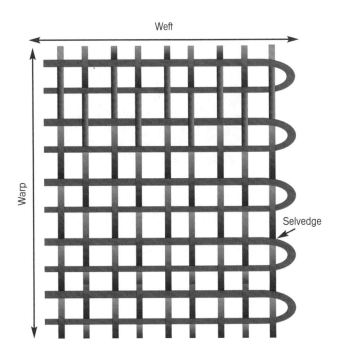

Fabrics

Type of Weave		Description
Plain Weave		• The simplest weave. • Creates an interlocking pattern. • The weft yarns pass over and under the warp yarns. • Examples include polyester, cotton and calico.
Twill Weave		• Creates a diagonal pattern (bias). • The weft yarns pass over and under either 2 or 4 warp yarns. • Examples include denim and gaberdine.
Satin Weave		• Creates a smooth, shiny fabric. • The weft yarns over and under 4–7 warp yarns • Often used for furnishings. • Examples include damask.
Jacquard Weave		• Creates a complex woven fabric. • Is made on a specialist loom – a Jacquard loom – that is often controlled by a computer. • Produces high quality fabrics that are very expensive. • Examples of end products include rich furnishings and formal wear, e.g. wedding waistcoats.
Pile Weave		• Creates a raised surface made of upright loops. • Examples include velvet, corduroy and terry towelling.

Pile Fabrics
Edexcel • OCR

Pile fabrics are woven or knitted fabrics that have **cut fibres or loops of yarn** standing **upright** from the surface, e.g. terry towelling or corduroy. When the upright fibres / loops are tightly-packed, it creates a 'plush' texture, e.g. velvet.

Pile fabrics have a **nap** – the direction in which the loops / fibres naturally lie.

Non-Woven Fabrics

Non-woven fabrics are made from **raw fibres** (usually synthetic), rather than yarns, by one of the following methods:

- using **chemicals** to **mat** the fibres together
- using **heat** to **bond** the fibres together
- **stitching** the fibres together in **layers**.

Non-woven fabrics…

- have no **grain**
- **don't stretch or fray** easily
- are **not as strong** or flexible as knitted and woven fabrics
- are **permeable**.

Wool felts   Edexcel • OCR

In **Wool felts** the fibres are matted together in the following way:

1. A **web** of fibres is laid on a belt.
2. The web is treated with a **solution**.
3. The web is heated.
4. The web is passed through a range of **mechanical rollers**.

Needle Felts   Edexcel • OCR

Needle felts are made in the following way:

1. Fibres are laid on top of each other
2. The fibres are passed through a series of **barbed needles**.

This process **drags** the **fibres** backwards and forwards and up and down, **interlocking** the fibres together.

Bonded Fabrics   Edexcel • OCR

Bonded fabrics are made by laying fibres across each other. This may be done randomly or in a specific way using **specialised machinery**. The fibres are **bonded** together to form webs using either:

- an **adhesive** to **glue** the fibres together
- a **solvent** to **soften** the fibres so they stick together
- **lines of stitching** – a cheap way of producing fabrics.

The webs are then layered and fused together, using heat, to create the final fabric.

Quick Test

1. What is the difference between natural fibres and synthetic fibres?
2. Weft is 'horizontal' and warp is 'vertical'. **True** or **false**?
3. Are knitted fabrics or woven fabrics most elastic and why?
4. What is the simplest type of weave?
5. How is heat used in the production of non-woven fabrics?

KEY WORDS

Make sure you understand these words before moving on!

- Fibres
- Worsted
- Woollen
- Elastic
- Weft
- Warp
- Knitted
- Woven
- Selvedge
- Bias
- Twill
- Satin
- Jacquard
- Pile fabrics
- Nap
- Bonded

Fabrics

Fabric	Description	Example
Rubber / **Latex**	Fine latex can be moulded and shaped into seamless clothing, e.g. wetsuits and clubwear.	
Net	A mesh-based material formed by twisting two ends of yarn together. It can be used for curtains and packaging.	
Lace	Machine-made lace is manufactured on a net base and used mainly for interior products and special garments, e.g. wedding dresses.	
Metals	Steel, copper and aluminium can be made into very thin yarns and used in fabrics, e.g. electronic 'smart' fabrics.	
Glass	Glass fibres have a reflective surface but are very abrasive (cause rubbing). They're used in specialist textiles for industrial and architectural products, e.g. fibreglass.	
Paper	Paper-like fabrics, e.g. Tyvek, are already being used for clothing.	
Ceramics	Ceramics can be combined with polyester fibres. They are waterproof, provide UV protection and can help to maintain body temperature. They're used for insulation and in specialist garments for extreme conditions.	

Choosing Fabrics

It's important for a designer to choose the best fabric for a job. They need to consider if the fabric needs to...
- be natural or synthetic based
- have high **abrasion** qualities, i.e. hard wearing
- be cool or warm to wear
- offer protection from wind or rain
- offer special protection e.g. against flames or heat.

Properties of Fabrics

Different fibres and fabrics have different properties (qualities). For example cotton is cool, wool is warm, and polyester dries quickly.

These properties need to be matched to the functions of the end product.

Designers use charts to help them do this (see p.42).

Mixing Properties of Fabrics

The properties of a yarn or fabric can be enhanced by combining different fibres. This is called a **blend** or a mixture.

Textile manufacturers blend fibres to produce yarns and fabrics with the combined properties of both fibres.

One of the best-known blends is polyester and cotton, called '**polycotton**'.

The mixing and blending of fibres also means that the end product can be cheaper to make and sell. Another well-known blend is polyester and wool.

Properties of Polycotton

Properties of Polyester
- very strong
- very durable
- high elasticity
- good insulation
- very cheap
- easy to care for
- very crease resistant

Combined Properties
- high strength
- high elasticity
- very cheap
- easy to care for
- crease resistant
- good insulation
- absorbent

Properties of Cotton
- durable
- good strength
- not very elastic
- absorbent
- not a good insulator
- very cheap
- easy to care for
- creases easily

Quick Test

1 What type of fabric could be used to make a seamless suit for open-water swimming?
2 Give two properties that ceramics can provide when combined with polyester fibres.
3 Give two advantages of mixing and blending fibres to produce a fabric.

KEY WORDS
Make sure you understand these words before moving on!
- Latex
- Abrasion
- Polycotton

Properties of Fibres and Fabrics

Properties of Fabrics

Fibre	Classification	Origin	Strength	Elasticity	Absorbency	Crease Resistance	Durability	Warmth	Flammability	General Description
Cotton	Natural / vegetable	Seed bolls of the cotton plant	★★★	★	★★★★	★	★★★★	★★	★★★	A cheap, strong but cooling fabric, which creases fairly easily. Used for denim, damask, piqué, gabardine, etc.
Wool	Natural / animal	Fleece from various animals, e.g. sheep	★★	★★★★	★★★★★	★★★	★★	★★★★★	★★★	A soft, hardwearing fabric that is unlikely to crease much. Used for flannel, jersey, serge, shetland and tweed.
Silk	Natural / animal	Cocoon produced by silk worm	★★★★	★★★	★★★★	★★★	★★★	★★★	★★★	An expensive fabric that is smooth to the touch and drapes well. Cooling. Used for chiffon, satin, taffeta.
Linen	Natural / vegetable	The stems of flax plants	★★★★	★	★★★★	★	★★★★	★★	★★★	Even stronger when wet, linen is very cooling but creases easily.
Viscose	Manufactured / regenerated	Cellulose extracted from wood pulp	★★	★	★★★★★	★★	★★	★★	★★	A cheap light material though not particularly strong. Very versatile and used in all sorts of clothing from lingerie to suits.
Acetate	Manufactured / regenerated	Cellulose extracted from wood pulp	★★	★	★★	★★	★	★★	★★	Like viscose, it is resistant to biological breakdown and very versatile.
Rayon	Manufactured / regenerated	Cellulose extracted from wood pulp	★★★	★	★★★★	★★★	★★	★★	★	Referred to as synthetic silk, used for lightweight clothing.
Polyester	Manufactured / synthetic	Chemicals from oil are polymerised, i.e. chemically joined.	★★★★	★★★	★	★★★	★★★★	★★	★★	A good all round synthetic, which is often blended with cotton to add crease resistance.
Nylon	Manufactured / synthetic	Chemicals from oil are polymerised	★★★★	★★★	★	★★★★	★★★★★	★★	★★	Like polyester it is strong and crease resistant. Its toughness makes it suitable for carpets.
Acrylic	Manufactured / synthetic	Manmade fibres derived from synthetic polymers	★★★	★★★	★	★★★	★★★	★★★★	★	A warm fabric used for jumpers and bedding.
Elastane, e.g. lycra	Manufactured / elastomeric / synthetic	Synthetic polymer (85% polyurethane)	★★★	★★★★★	★	★★★	★★★	★★	★	A durable fibre used in sportswear, leggings and jeans
Microfibres	Manufactured / synthetic	Chemicals from oil are polymerised	★★★★	★★★	★★★	★★★	★★★	★★★	★★	These tiny fibres can be woven so closely that they can prevent penetration by water, whilst allowing the fabric to 'breathe'.

Key:
★★★★★ = excellent
★ = poor

Other properties or factors to be considered when looking at fibres and their properties are:
- **Wearability** – How does the fabric feel when it is worn? Does it drape well?
- **Comfort** – How comfortable is the fabric when worn next to the skin?
- **Launderability** – How well it can be washed, maintained and cared for? You need to know fibre origins in order to know how to care for the product once it is made.
- **Safety** – Are there any safety issues to be considered when using this fabric?

Other attributes to be considered are the visual impact (how it looks) and the aesthetic quality (the design) of the fabrics.

N.B. The above table is generic and based on data from various sources. Some fabrics can be successful at any of the properties listed if properly treated.

Properties of Fibres and Fabrics

Making Use of Special Properties

To make them **more useful** to manufacturers, some fabrics can have…

- their **properties enhanced**
- special properties **built–in**
- special properties added **after construction** of a product.

Special Properties

The following fibres and fabrics all have special properties:

Elastane…

- has a lot of **extension** or elasticity (stretch)
- can improve the comfort and appearance of a fabric
- uses include sportswear, underwear and suits
- includes Lycra® from Dupont.

Recycled and biodegradable fibres…

- are made from recycled plastic bottles (PTFE or PET)
- are used to produce lightweight, **breathable** fabrics
- are used in fleeces (e.g. Polartech and Patagonia)
- are biodegradable due to the way they are processed.

Kevlar® (aramid)…

- is extremely hardwearing and five times stronger than steel
- can be stiffened or softened using chemicals
- is used in protective clothing and bullet-proof vests.

Fabrics with a membrane…

- are able to control which substances pass through them
- include **Gore-Tex®** and **Sympatex®**, which are waterproof but breathable
- are used in outdoor clothing.

BioSteel…

- is a very strong fibre-based material
- is a genetically modified fibre containing casein from goats' milk and protein silk from spiders' webs
- is used in recyclable bullet-proof vests.

Nomex®…

- has insulating properties
- is used where heat and flame resistance is needed
- is used in firefighters' uniforms.

Microfibres…

- are small, fine fibres up to 60 times finer than human hair
- are normally made from polyamide or polyester fibres, e.g. Tactel.

Quick Test

1. Name two fabrics that are highly absorbent.
2. Name two fabrics that have very little elasticity.
3. Suggest one fabric you might use if you wanted to make a garment that was exceptionally warm.
4. Name two fabrics that are used for bullet-proof vests because of their exceptional strength.
5. What is the key property of Nomex?

KEY WORDS

Make sure you understand these words before moving on!

- Absorbency
- Durability
- Elastane
- Extension
- Breathable
- Kevlar®
- Gore-Tex®
- Sympatex®
- Nomex®

Finishes

Applying Finishes

Textile products often have **finishes** applied to them to...

- **protect** the fabric or design features
- change the **feel** of the fabric
- improve **resilience** and **durability**
- improve the **appearance** of the fabric
- **add value** to the product.

There are three types of finish:

- **physical finishes**
- **biological finishes**
- **chemical** finishes.

Finishes can be **applied** at **different stages** of the production process. They can **increase the cost** of a product, so there must be a good reason for using one.

The production / manufacturing specification should include clear instructions about...

- **what** finish to apply
- **when** to apply the finish.

Physical Finishes   Edexcel • OCR

Process		Effect	Suitable Fabrics	Products
Brushing		• Fabrics are passed through a series of wire rollers. • The fabric is left soft and fluffy.	• Can be applied to cotton, wool, polyester and polyamide.	• Applications include bedding and fleeces.
Calendering		• Fabrics are passed between heated rollers. • This gives the fabric a smooth finish.	• Can be applied to cotton and wool.	• Applications include chintz fabric for furnishing.
Laminating		• Layers of fabric are bonded together using heat or adhesive. • Produces layers of fabrics with different properties.	• Can be applied to cotton and polyester.	• Applications include table cloths, aprons, outdoor clothing.

Biological Finishes Edexcel

Biostoning…

- uses a cellulose enzyme which acts on the fabric (an alternative to rubbing with pumice)
- produces a 'worn' look and a softer feel
- can be applied to cotton (denim), Tencel and Lyocell
- applications include clothing, e.g. jeans.

Biopolishing…

- uses an enzyme which acts on the fabric
- adds a sheen to the fabric, softens it and reduces pilling
- can be applied to cotton and Tencel
- applications include leisure clothing.

Chemical Finishes

Mercerising…

- involves the fabric being placed in a sodium hydroxide solution
- causes the fibres to swell and become more shiny, absorbent and strong
- can be applied to cotton
- applications include clothing, e.g. shirts.

Waterproofing or water repelling finishes…

- involve a silicon-based chemical being sprayed onto the fabric
- provide a water repellent layer
- can be applied to all fabrics
- are applied to many products including outdoor clothing and tents.

Flame-proofing…

- chemicals are applied to the yarn or fabric
- provides a protective layer that slows down the burning process
- can be applied to cotton, linen and rayon.
- applications include interior fabrics and furnishings.

Finishes

Chemical Finishes (Cont.)

Anti-static finishes…

- involve a chemical based product being applied to the fabric
- stop the build up of electrostatic charge
- can be applied to synthetics, acetate and silk
- have many applications including underwear and carpets.

Anti-felting finish…

- is an oxidative treatment that is applied to the fabric
- softens rough fibres preventing matting and felting whilst retaining warmth
- can be applied to wool
- applications include clothing, e.g. pull-overs.

Bleaching…

- uses a strong chemical, which is applied to the yarn or fabric
- removes all natural colour but can weaken the fabric
- can be applied to cotton and linen
- applications include most cotton products, e.g. clothing and bedding.

Crease resistance…

- involves a resin being applied to the fabric and then heat-cured (set)
- uses the layer of resin to prevent creasing
- can be applied to cotton, linen and rayon fabrics
- applications include clothing, e.g. suits.

Shrink resistance…

- involves a resin based finish, or chlorine-based chemical treatment, being applied to the fabric
- stops the fabric from shrinking so it can be machine washed
- can be applied to wool
- applications include clothing, e.g. trousers.

Unbleached Cotton

Bleached Cotton

Other Finishes

AQA • OCR

Some finishes have been developed for specialist applications. Products cannot claim to have these properties on their labels unless they have been fully tested against a set of standards (see page 68).

Type of Resistance	Description
Spark	• Protects against spark discharge. • Used in industrial settings. • Applications include protective clothing for emergency services, military products and manufacturing operators.
Fire	• Fabrics can withstand certain fire conditions. • Applications include interior products and protective clothing for emergency services.
Cut, Tear, Ballistic	• Fabrics designed to protect the user in industry or sporting events. • Applications include body armour and specialist clothing for the emergency services, sports people and industrial workers.
Abrasion	• Prevents wear and tear of the garment. • Applications include body armour, protective clothing for emergency services, clothing and sportswear.

Quick Test

1 What are the active agents used in biological finishing?
2 What effect does calendering have on the fabric?
3 What type of fibre is an anti-felting finish usually applied to?
4 How is a water-repellent finish achieved?
5 Give one advantage and one disadvantage of bleaching.

KEY WORDS
Make sure you understand these words before moving on!
• Resilience
• Physical finishes
• Biological finishes
• Anti-static
• Bleaching

Components

Components

When creating a textile product, various **components** can be used with fabric to...

- **enhance** or **embellish**
- add **functionality**.

You should consider the end-user when selecting components, e.g. hook and loop fastenings are easier for young children to use than buckles or buttons.

Component	Description
Dyes	Dyes are used to colour yarns or fabrics: • **Natural fibres** – **reactive dyes** and **acid dyes** • **Synthetic fibres** – **disperse dyes**.
Inks	There is a range of natural and synthetic inks used in textiles. They are normally used to **draw** onto the fabric.
Paints	Different types of paint are available for... • creating **special effects**, e.g. 3D textures • painting **specific fabrics**, e.g. silk.
Elastics	Elastics are used in textiles for different purposes, including... • to **hold fabrics in place** and to create **flexible openings** • for **embroidery** and **special effects**.
Threads	There is a range of sewing machine threads available. You can select threads depending on the **fabric** and the **end use** of the product. **Hand embroidery threads** are used for **decorative work**.
Knitting Yarns	Knitting yarns are available, for hand and machine knitting, in **different weights** and **thicknesses**. They can be made of **different fibres**, including wool and polyester.
Fastenings	There are a range of fastenings that can be used, including **buttons**, **zips**, **hook and eye** fasteners, **press-studs**, poppers, toggles, parachute clips and **hook and loop** fastening, e.g. Velcro®.
Bindings	Bindings are available in different colours and are usually described as '**narrow fabrics**'. They can be used in a decorative and / or functional way.
Interfacings	**Interfacings** are used to **reinforce** or **add stability** to fabrics. They are often **applied using heat**, i.e. they are an example of a fusible material.

Collins Revision

GCSE
D&T Textiles
Technology
ESSENTIALS

GCSE D&T

Textiles Technology

Controlled Assessment Guide

About this Guide

The new GCSE Design & Technology courses are assessed through…
- written exam papers
- controlled assessment.

This guide provides…
- an overview of how your course is assessed
- an explanation of controlled assessment
- advice on how best to demonstrate your knowledge and skills in the controlled assessment.

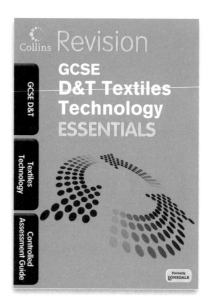

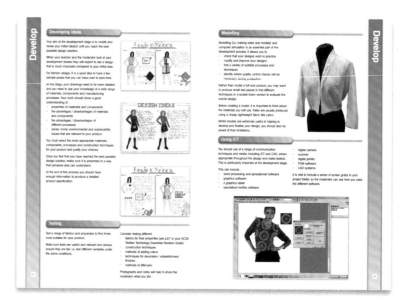

What is Controlled Assessment?

Controlled assessment has replaced coursework. It involves completing a 'design and make' task (two separate tasks for OCR) within a set number of hours.

Your exam board will provide you with a range of tasks to choose from. The purpose of the task(s) is to see how well you can bring together all your skills and knowledge together to design and make an original textiles product.

You must produce individual work under controlled conditions, i.e. under the supervision of a teacher.

Your teacher can review your work and give you general feedback. However, all the work must be your own.

How is Controlled Assessment Marked?

Your teacher will mark your work using guidelines from the exam board. A moderator at the exam board will review these marks to ensure that they are fair.

You will not just be marked on the quality of your end product – the other stages of design and development are just as important, if not more so!

At each stage of the task(s), it is essential to clearly communicate…
- what you did
- how you did it
- why you did it.

Contents

This guide looks at the main stages you will need to go through in your controlled assessment task(s), providing helpful tips and advice along the way.

Exam Board	Course	Written Paper	Controlled Assessment
AQA	Full Course	• 2 hours • 120 marks • 40% of total marks Section A (30 marks) – A design question based on a context which you will be notified of before the exam Section B (90 marks) – Covers all the content on the specification, i.e. all the material covered in your Essentials Revision Guide.	• Approx. 45 hours • 90 marks • 60% of total marks
Edexcel	Full Course	• 1 hour 30 minutes • 80 marks • 40% of total marks	• Approx. 40 hours • 100 marks • 60% of total marks The 'design and make' activities can be linked (combined design and make) or separate (design one product, make another).
OCR	Short Course and Full Course (Yr 1)	**Sustainable Design:** • 1 hour • 60 marks • 20% of total marks (40% of short course) Section A – 15 short answer questions. Section B – 3 questions that may involve sketching, annotation, short sentences or more extended writing.	**Introduction to Designing and Making:** • 20 hours • 60 marks • 30% of total marks (60% of short course)
	Full Course (Yr 2)	**Technical Aspects of Designing and Making:** • 1 hour 15 minutes • 60 marks • 20% of total marks Section A – 3 questions based on the technical aspects of working with materials, tools and equipment. Section B – 2 questions on the design of products reflecting the wider aspects of sustainability and human use. One of these questions will require a design response.	**Making Quality Products:** • 20 hours • 60 marks • 30% of total marks

Important Considerations

Unlike your teacher, the moderator will not have the opportunity to see how you progress with the task. They will not be able to talk to you or ask questions – they must make their assessment based on the evidence you provide. That means it is essential to communicate your thoughts, ideas and decisions clearly at each stage of the process:

- Organise your folder so the work is in a **logical** order.
- Ensure that text is **legible** and that spelling, punctuation and grammar are accurate.
- Use an **appropriate** form and style of writing.
- Make sure you use technical terms correctly.

Because you only have a limited amount of time, it is essential to plan ahead. Below are suggested times for each of the stages.

You should produce your own more detailed time plan, dividing the total time for each stage between the individual tasks. However, it is important to remember that all the different stages are part of a continuous development process – timings are for guidance only, to help you make sure you spend a majority of your time working on the areas worth the most marks.

At the end of the controlled assessment you will need to submit the final product (or a photograph of it) along with a concise design folder. You should aim to produce about 20 x A3 sheets for your folder (10 for a short course or for separate design and make tasks). An equivalent amount of A4 sheets or electronic files may be acceptable – check with your teacher.

AQA award up to 6 marks for clarity of presentation throughout your folder. Whilst these marks are important, 84 of the total 90 marks are for the content, so make good use of your time – don't waste time creating elaborate borders and titles!

Stage	Tasks	AQA Marks	AQA Guideline Time (Hr)	OCR Marks	OCR Guideline Time (Hr)	Edexcel Marks	Edexcel Guideline Time (Hr)
Investigate	Analysing the brief	8	4	29	6½	15	5
	Research						
	Design specification						
Design	Initial ideas	32	16	61	13½	20	7
	Reviewing ideas						
Develop	Developing ideas					15	8
Plan	Product specification			55	12	6	2
	Production plan						
Make	Making product	32	16			38	16
Test and evaluate	Testing and evaluation	12	6	35	8	6	2
Communicate*	Clarity of communication	6	3	0	0	0	0
Total		**90**	**45**	**180**	**40**	**100**	**40**

Analysing the Task

To get the maximum marks, you need to…
- analyse the task / brief in detail
- clearly identify all the design needs.

It is a good idea to start by writing out the task / brief…
- as it is written by the exam board
- in your own words (to make sure you understand what you're being asked to do).

Highlight the key words and phrases and make sure you understand them.

You should then identify any specific issues that you need to consider before you can start designing the product.

Ask yourself the following questions:
- Who will use the end product?
- What will it be used for?
- Where will it be used?
- What sort of shop/retail outlet will it be sold through?
- Are there any cost restrictions that will influence my design?
- How many products would be made if it went into commercial production?

Make sure you have clear answers to all the above before you go any further.

You do not need to write an essay. You could use…
- an attribute analysis table
- a mind map
- a spider diagram
- a list of bullet points
- a short piece of written work.

At this stage it is a good idea to…
- eliminate all the things that you don't need
- make a list of all the questions that you need to answer before you can begin designing
- decide what method of research is needed to answer each question.

TASK ANALYSIS

Materials and fabrics - what materials are going to be used? Fabric tests will need to be conducted to see whether they could be used on a range of garments. Look at the fabrics that were around during these eras. How much did the fabric cost?

Decorations: what decoration(s) are going to suit the garment? The accessories would also be chosen according to where the garment will be worn eg a hat is appropriate for a wedding. What type of shoes can be worn? What about hairstyles and jewellery?

Who would have used it? - What type of people would it be worn by- younger/older generation. When would it be worn? - special occasion, business wear or just as casual wear. Could the garment be dressed up or down with a combination of tops?

Cost/size: The total cost of the garment should be kept to a minimum. The size will vary according to different sizes of people. The garment should be appropriate for individual shapes. The age groups should be considered along with the lengths of the garments.

Design a range of clothes based on a popular cult from one of these eras. Design a range of male and female clothes and accessories typical of one of these fashion cults. Select and make up one of your designs.

Construction methods: Make a construction plan to show what you plan to do and in stages. Note the equipment used. Identify the construction methods - sizes of stitches. Comment on the type of cut.

Colour schemes: Look at the colours that were in fashion during each eras. Moodboards can be created. Use similar shapes which were available during the era(s)

Fashion in the 60's and 70's - Research into the two eras. Who set the trends? What was produced on the catwalks? What were the street wears? Find out about the fashion trends that existed and who started these trends?

Influences: who were the influences? Research into the types of music that were around during the two eras (60's + 70's). The connection between fashion and Hollywood. Find out about TV and its influences on fashion. The attitudes of younger generation eg in 1960's

Research

Because you don't have very long to conduct your research, you need to make sure it is all relevant. It should help you to make decisions about all the issues that you identified in your task analysis, so these are the areas to focus on.

Make sure you keep accurate records. You will need to refer back to the information throughout the task.

You should know about the different research methods used in commercial design, but be aware that they may not be appropriate to your design task because of the limited time available to you. Possibly the most useful types of research that you can carry out are...
*   an interview with the client / end-user to find out their requirements
*   analysis of existing products.

Product Analysis

Product analysis is the process of disassembling (taking apart) existing products to find out what they are made from and how they are made. You should identify...
*   the key functions
*   the key design features
*   the fabrics used, their fibre content and method of construction
*   how many pattern pieces were used
*   all the components used
*   the construction methods used
*   the method of colour application
*   any techniques used to decorate, embellish or manipulate the fabrics
*   any finishes used
*   any legal or BSI standards that apply
*   what aftercare and maintenance is needed
*   any environmental issues associated with making or using the product.

You should also consider...
*   whether the product is appropriate for its target market
*   what ergonomic considerations would have influenced the design
*   what anthropometric measurements were required to make the product
*   what method of manufacture would have been used
*   the lifecycle of the product
*   whether the product can be recycled
*   the effect of the product on our lifestyle
*   whether the product is inclusive (or whether some groups of people won't be able to use it).

As part of your product analysis you might also want to get feedback from consumers:
*   What do they like about it?
*   What don't they like about it?
*   Is it good value for money?
*   What improvements would they like to see made?

The purpose of product analysis is to help you produce a product that is better than those already available. It should help you to identify...
*   desirable / successful features (features you could incorporate into your design)
*   undesirable / unsuccessful features (features to avoid in your design)
*   areas for improvement (areas that you should try to improve upon in your design, e.g. reducing cost, making the product sustainable).

Interviews, Questionnaires and Surveys

Interviews, questionnaires and surveys normally rely on a large sample group to produce reliable data.

It is fine to adapt these methods for your task – targeting a small, specific group or individual and producing a product that meets their particular needs – as long as you show that you understand the pros and cons of doing this in your evaluation.

Research Summary

It is essential to summarise your findings and explain how the data gathered through your research will assist you. You should record…

- what you did
- why you did it
- what you hoped to find out (what your expectations were)
- what you actually found out
- how these findings will affect your design ideas.

The results can be displayed using…

- tables, pie charts, star profiles, line graphs, pictographs and bar charts (ICT or hand drawn)
- a mood board combined with notes to sum up the key points.

Make sure you list all the secondary sources you used, e.g. website, books, magazines, etc. in a bibliography.

Design Specification

Your design specification should list all the things that need to be included in your design with details of any restrictions you must observe. It should…

- relate directly to the brief
- reflect the findings of your research
- be clearly presented (usually as a list of bullet points)
- be realistic and achievable.

You need to be clear about…

- the essential design criteria, i.e. the criteria that must be met to ensure the product is fit for purpose
- the desirable design criteria, i.e. criteria that are not essential but would improve / enhance the product.

You should be able to justify all the criteria on your specification using findings from your research.

Example

Brief: A Children's wear company wants a range of summer clothes for children aged 3–6 years old with a 'Jungle' theme.

The logo / pattern needs to be based on a jungle

NB: It is important to remember that for many children's products, although the child is the end-user, it is the parent who buys the product.

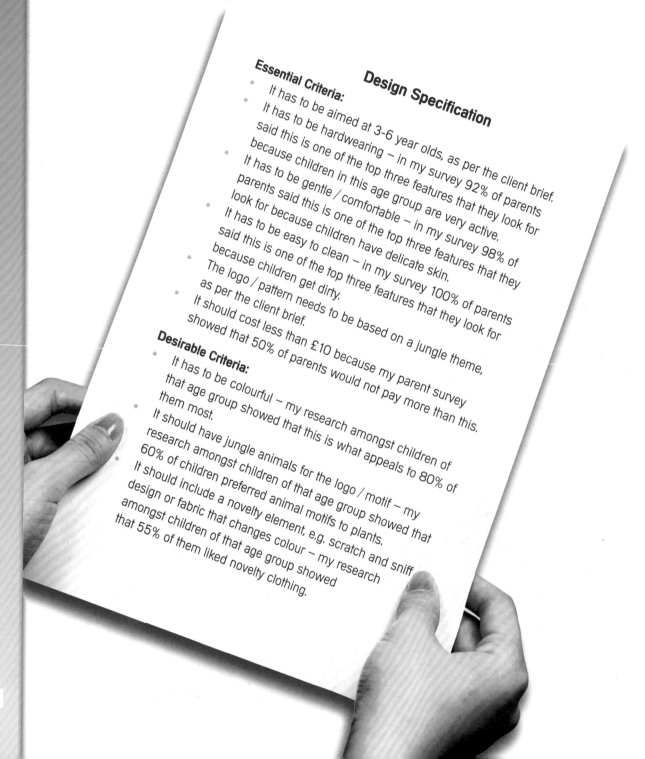

Design Specification

Essential Criteria:

- It has to be aimed at 3-6 year olds, as per the client brief.
- It has to be hardwearing – in my survey 92% of parents said this is one of the top three features that they look for because children in this age group are very active.
- It has to be gentle / comfortable – in my survey 98% of parents said this is one of the top three features that they look for because children have delicate skin.
- It has to be easy to clean – in my survey 100% of parents said this is one of the top three features that they look for because children get dirty.
- The logo / pattern needs to be based on a jungle theme, as per the client brief.
- It should cost less than £10 because my parent survey showed that 50% of parents would not pay more than this.

Desirable Criteria:

- It has to be colourful – my research amongst children of that age group showed that this is what appeals to 80% of them most.
- It should have jungle animals for the logo / motif – my research amongst children of that age group showed that 60% of children preferred animal motifs to plants.
- It should include a novelty element, e.g. scratch and sniff design or fabric that changes colour – my research amongst children of that age group showed that 55% of them liked novelty clothing.

Initial Ideas

Generating ideas is an important part of any design process, and you should allow yourself plenty of time for this stage. This is your chance to show off your creative skills, but make sure your ideas...

- are realistic and workable
- address all the essential criteria on your design specification.

At this stage, the key areas to explore are...

- shape
- colour
- pattern
- texture
- decoration / embellishment
- size and proportion
- fabrics
- construction.

You are expected to use a variety of graphic techniques including ICT and CAD, so try using...

- quick sketching techniques to get your initial ideas on paper
- techniques such as 'rubbing' to experiment with texture
- graphics software to create different motifs, colourways, geometric patterns and repeat patterns
- a digital camera or scanner to manipulate images.

Presenting Ideas

You need to present your initial ideas clearly, but remember there are no extra marks for 'pretty'.

To communicate your design ideas clearly and show how they relate to the criteria on your design specification, make sure you use notes and annotations alongside your drawings.

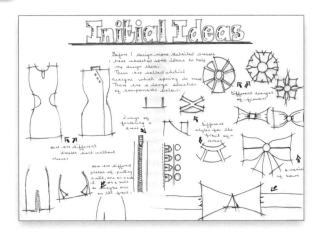

Reviewing Ideas

You need to review your initial ideas to select one or two to develop further.

They must satisfy the essential criteria on your design specification, but you will also want to consider...

- which designs satisfy the most desirable criteria
- which designs are most unique / innovative
- which designs are most appealing / attractive.

Ask your client / end-user for their opinion – which ones would they buy?

Developing Ideas

Your aim at the development stage is to modify and revise your initial idea(s) until you reach the best possible design solution.

When your teacher and the moderator look at your development sheets they will expect to see a design that is much improved compared to your initial idea.

For fashion design, it is a good idea to have a few sample poses that you can trace over to save time.

At this stage, your drawings need to be more detailed and you need to use your knowledge of a wide range of materials, components and manufacturing processes. Your work should show a good understanding of…

- properties of materials and components
- the advantages / disadvantages of materials and components
- the advantages / disadvantages of different processes
- social, moral, environmental and sustainability issues that are relevant to your product.

You must select the most appropriate materials, components, processes and construction techniques for your product and justify your choices.

Once you feel that you have reached the best possible design solution, make sure it is presented in a way that someone else can understand.

At the end of this process you should have enough information to produce a detailed product specification.

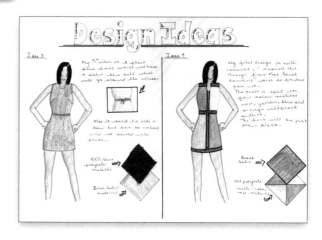

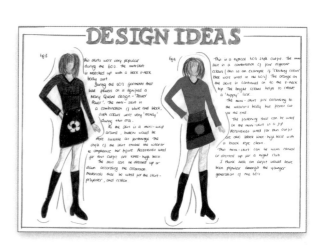

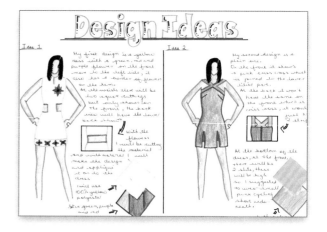

Testing

Test a range of fabrics and processes to find those most suitable for your product.

Make sure tests are useful and relevant and always ensure they are fair, i.e. test different variables under the same conditions.

Consider testing different…

- fabrics for their properties (see p.67 or your GCSE Textiles Technology Essentials Revision Guide)
- construction techniques
- methods of adding colour
- techniques for decoration / embellishment
- finishes
- methods of aftercare.

Photographs and notes will help to show the moderator what you did.

Modelling

Modelling (i.e. making toiles and models) and computer simulation is an essential part of the development process. It allows you to…

- check that your designs work in practice
- modify and improve your designs
- trial a variety of suitable processes and techniques
- identify where quality control checks will be necessary during production.

Rather than model a full-size product, you may want to produce small test pieces to trial different techniques or a scaled down version to evaluate the overall design.

Before creating a model, it is important to think about the materials you will use. Toiles are usually produced using a cheap, lightweight fabric like calico.

Whilst models are extremely useful in helping to develop and finalise your design, you should also be aware of their limitations.

Using ICT

You should use of a range of communication techniques and media, including ICT and CAD, where appropriate throughout the design and make task(s). This is particularly important at the development stage.

This can include…

- word processing and spreadsheet software
- graphics software
- a graphics tablet
- specialised textiles software
- digital camera
- scanner
- digital printer
- PDM software
- CAD systems.

It is vital to include a series of screen grabs in your project folder, so the moderator can see how you used the different software.

Product Specification

A product specification contains instructions and information that will be used to make prototype and sample products.

It is important that the information is accurate and clear, as it will be used to calculate the cost of your product.

Your product specification will contain the following:
- a working drawing of your product – a black and white technical drawing of your product showing…
  – front and back views
  – measurement details
  – exploded drawings, highlighting key details
  – details of seams, etc.

- a written description of the product, including…
  – a list of all the materials and components to be used
  – amounts / quantities needed
  – fabric swatches and samples
- sizing details for all components and pieces of the product
- appropriate care label information and instructions for maintenance.

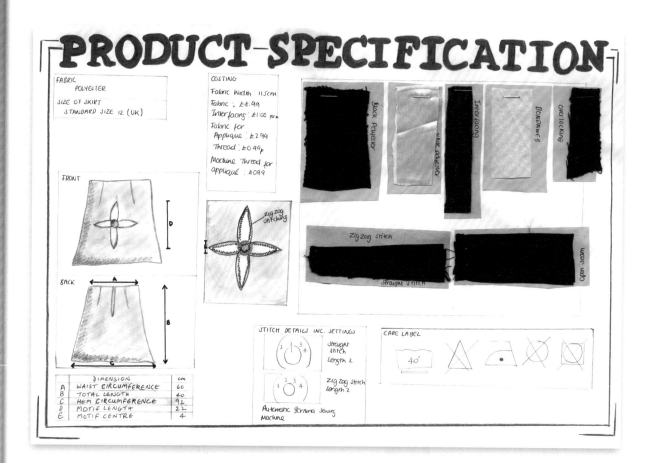

Pattern Making

You will need a pattern before you can make your product.

There are different ways of creating a pattern:
- disassemble an existing product
- use a commercial pattern
- use standard pattern blocks
- use pattern generation software.

Once you have created a pattern you need to check that it works by making a toile. You can then identify any modifications that need to be made to the pattern before making the actual product.

Manufacturing Specification

Your manufacturing specification should provide you (or someone else) with a list of guidelines to follow during the production process.

Your manufacturing specification must include...
- a description of the fabric to be used and how it must be treated
- a list of components needed
- a list of tools required
- a detailed description of the processes involved, e.g. cutting, machining, pressing
- the details of the pattern to be used
- the quality control checks you want to put in place
- a detailed production plan (you can use a flow chart for this).

You might also want to include...
- set time lines and guides for each stage of manufacture, e.g. a Gantt chart
- details of the critical points in the making process
- details of possible problems that could occur and how they can be corrected.

If you use a flow chart to show your production plan, there are different, specific symbols for each stage of the process. Some are shown here:

Flow Chart Symbols

Terminator
Represents start, restart and stop.

Process
Represents a particular instruction or action.

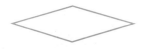

Decision
Represents a choice that can lead to another pathway.

Input / Output
Represents additions to / removals from a particular process.

The symbols are linked together by arrows to show the correct sequence of events.

You should aim to keep your flow chart as clear and simple as possible.

Example

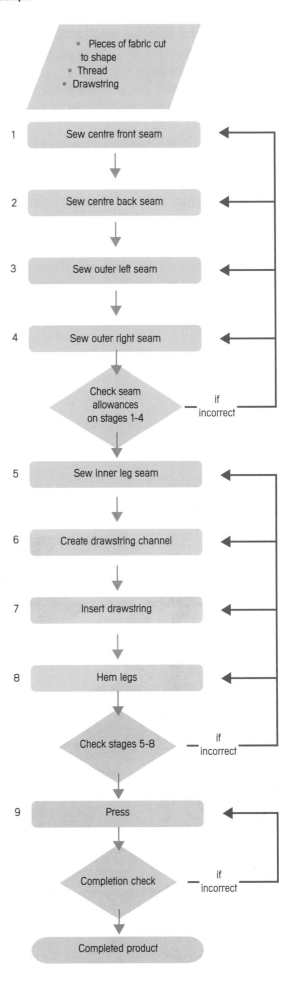

Manufacture

Making the final product is an important part of your controlled assessment. It is essential that you…

- follow your manufacturing specification
- use all equipment correctly and safely, following health and safety guidelines
- use a range of skills and techniques
- use the correct pattern annotation when laying out pattern pieces
- make use of CAM where appropriate (but at least 50% of your work should be manual to demonstrate your skills)
- make your product as carefully as possible
- ensure that you carry out quality control checks
- correct errors or mistakes as they arise.

Remember, all the materials, methods and processes that you choose must help to make your product the best possible design solution for the brief. Don't include something just to show off your skills!

The finished product should be…

- accurately assembled
- well finished
- fully functional.

Don't worry if it doesn't turn out quite the way you hoped though - you will earn marks for all the skills and processes you demonstrate, so make sure you record them all clearly in your folder.

You must include a photograph of the end product and it is a good idea to include photographs of the various stages of production too.

Health and Safety

Before you begin making your product, always carry out a risk assessment.

Look at each stage of your production plan in turn and make a list of possible health and safety risks.

Work back through the list and plan how you will minimise the risks at each stage, e.g. by wearing the correct protective clothing, by ensuring you know how to use the equipment correctly, etc.

Industry

You should have a good understanding of the methods and processes used in the textile design and manufacturing industry.

Although you will probably only produce one final product, it is important to show that you are aware of various possible methods of production and how your product would be manufactured commercially. You should explain this in your project folder.

If your product could potentially be manufactured using several different methods, try to list the pros and cons for each method and then use these lists to make a decision about which method you would recommend.

If you know that a method or process you are using to make your product would be carried out differently in a factory, make a note of this in your project folder – this will show your teacher and moderator how much you know!

Testing

Tests need to be carried out to check the performance and / or quality of the final product and ensure it meets all the criteria on your original design specification.

Tests do not have to be complicated. They just need to be sensible and helpful, e.g. test the usability and functionality of the product.

Keeping records is very important. In your project folder you need to…

- explain what tests were carried out
- explain why the tests were carried out

- describe what you found out
- explain what modifications you would make based on the test results
- include a photo of your product in use.

You should not test your product to destruction, but it is a good idea to take photos of your product before testing begins just in case anything goes wrong.

Evaluation

Evaluation is an ongoing process. During the design and development process, every decision you made (providing it is clearly justified) and all the client / end-user feedback counts towards your evaluation.

The final evaluation should summarise all your earlier conclusions and provide an objective evaluation of the final product.

When carrying out an evaluation, you should…

- refer back to the brief
- cross-check the end product against the original specification
- obtain client comments and feedback
- take a photograph of the client using the product
- carry out a simple end-user survey.

You need to establish…

- if the manufacturing techniques used were effective
- if the control systems and quality control checks you put in place were effective

- if the product meets all the criteria on the original brief and specifications
- if the product is easy to use
- if the product functions the way it was intended to
- what consumers think of the style of the product
- if consumers like / dislike any features
- if consumers would purchase the product and what they would be prepared to pay for it
- what consumers think the advantages and disadvantages of your product are compared to similar products
- what impact making and using the product has on the environment.

Depending on what you find out, you can include suggestions for further modifications in your evaluation.

Honesty is the best policy when writing evaluations. If something didn't work, say so – but always suggest a way of preventing the same problem in future.

Smart Materials and Technical Textiles

Technical Textiles

Technical textiles are manufactured for **functionality** and **technical performance**. The visual **appearance** is **less important**.

Technical textiles are used in many industries, including…
- Aerospace
- Medicine
- Military
- Health and Safety
- Transport
- GeoTextiles.

Traditional Textiles for Modern Living

The **properties** of **traditional fabrics** and **fibres** can often be **improved** to meet the demands of modern living by using **new treatments** and **technical finishes**.

Technical Tweed (from Musto®) is made of 95% wool and 5% nylon. It's given a high twist and a water repellant Teflon® finish to reduce pilling (bobbles) and water absorption.

Technical Tweed

Smart Materials

Smart materials are materials that can either…
- **respond to external stimuli**, e.g. extreme temperatures
- be activated by **internal or external power sources**.

Often smart technology can be **applied** to textiles **using traditional processes**, for example…
- embroidery with **photochromic threads** / dyeing with **thermochromic dyes** to produce products that **change colour with light** (photochromic) / **heat** (thermochromic) intensity
- embroidered images and text combined with **electronics** to create soft cushions or pillows that function as **keyboards** or **remote controls**
- fabrics on car seats that are embedded with **interactive panels**, **memory features** and embroidered or printed **controls**.

Smart textiles can be divided into the following areas:
- **Conductive textiles**
- **Power assisted textiles**
- **Communication textiles**
- **Medical textiles**.

Thermochromic Material

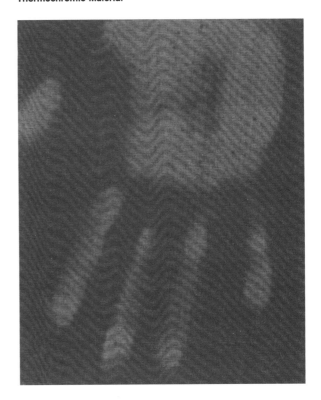

Smart Materials and Technical Textiles

Wearable Technology (Conductive Textiles) — Edexcel • OCR

Electrical circuits can be incorporated into textile fabrics using **fibres of conductive materials** such as carbon, steel, nickel and silver. These can be applied by…

- printing
- weaving
- knitting
- layering.

They also need a **power source** and **controls**, which can be embroidered or printed onto the fabric.

This technology has many practical uses such as…

- **temperature controlled** clothing
- blankets
- **soft interfaces**.

A soft interface is a **control**, like a key board or number pad. It's **made from pliable, soft material**. Textile fabrics are the materials of choice because of their flexibility and feel.

Power Assisted Textiles — Edexcel

Power assisted textiles **incorporate a power source**, which can be used to **power or control other products**, e.g. portable MP3 players or mobile phones.

There are three different types of power source:

Solar panels…

- draw **power from the Sun**
- can be incorporated into products such as backpacks and jackets.

Flexible batteries…

- can be applied to a variety of textiles surfaces
- can be **combined with other technology**, e.g. flexible switches that enable the product to be switched on from any angle or part.

Human force…

- uses **kinetic (movement) energy** and / or heat energy from the body as a power source (usually in combination with either solar panels or flexible batteries).

Solar Panels

Communication Textiles — Edexcel

Technological devices, e.g. infrared sensors, transmitters, MP3 systems and GPS systems, can be **incorporated into textiles** to…

- **protect** the user
- allow the user to **communicate** with others
- provide **entertainment**, e.g. recorded music / radio.

Communication textiles have many **health and safety applications**, e.g. they can be incorporated into sports wear (e.g. ski suits) and military uniforms to help locate people quickly in emergency situations.

Smart Materials and Technical Textiles

Medical Textiles Edexcel

Medical textiles **aid healing** or **monitor health** in different ways.

Microencapsulation incorporates **tiny bubbles** containing scents or chemicals into materials, which **burst when friction** or **heat is applied**, e.g. bandages that release drugs to promote healing.

Electronic sensors can be incorporated into a textile product to **monitor body temperature**, **moisture levels** or **pulse rate**, e.g. the LifeShirt® Clinical (plugs into a computer via a data cable, enabling a health care worker to monitor the patients vital signs).

Sanitised fabrics are fabrics that have been treated so that they are free from allergens and resistant to dust-mites, fungal growth and bacteria. They are often used in hospitals.

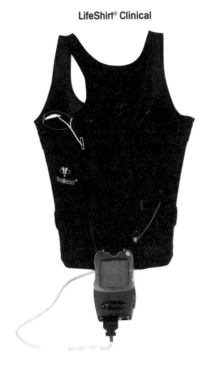

LifeShirt® Clinical

Nanotechnology

Nanoparticles are **microscopic particles** with **specific physical and chemical properties**.

Nanoparticles can be incorporated into **fabrics** to **enhance or change** their **properties**, for example…

- dyeability
- tensile strength
- resistance to abrasion
- resistance to flames / heat
- ability to repel water / soil.

NanoGrain® is the trade name for commercial **nanomaterials** produced by one company in this way.

Nanotubes or nanothreads are microscopic structures that can **conduct electricity and heat**. These have many applications in medical textiles.

Quick Test

1. What do thermochromic dyes do?
2. Name two conductive materials that can be used to incorporate electrical circuits into fabrics.
3. Name three practical uses for conductive textiles.
4. Name two products solar panels might be incorporated into.
5. Name two things that can be incorporated into textiles to aid healing or monitor health.

KEY WORDS

Make sure you understand these words before moving on!

- Interfacing
- Photochromic
- Thermochromic
- Conductive materials
- Power assisted
- Solar panels
- Kinetic
- Microencapsulation
- Nanomaterials

Practice Questions

1 What is another name for…

a) short fibres? ....

b) long fibres? ....

2 Name the two sources of natural fibres.

a) ....

b) ....

3 Which of the following are synthetic fibres? Tick the correct options.

A Cotton ☐   **B** Acrylic ☐

C Mohair ☐   **D** Hemp ☐

E Polyester ☐   **F** Silk ☐

4 Name four different ways of constructing fabrics.

a) ....   **b)** ....

c) ....   **d)** ....

5 Briefly explain the difference between weft and warp knitting.

....

....

6 Draw lines between the boxes to match each type of weave to the correct description.

Jacquard		Creates an interlocking pattern
Plain		Creates a smooth, shiny fabric.
Satin		Creates a complex woven fabric.

7 Fill in the missing words to complete the following sentences.

.... fibres like viscose, lyocell, acetate, cupro, modal, tencel are made from a

combination of .... and cellulose waste.

8 Which of the following statements about knitted fabrics are true? Tick the correct options.

    A They are made from yarn in a series of interlocking loops. ◯

    B They fray easily when cut. ◯

    C They are warm and can be improved by a finishing process called napping or brushing. ◯

    D Examples of end products include rich furnishings and formal wear, e.g. wedding waistcoats. ◯

    E It is a cheap way of producing fabrics. ◯

9 Is the following statement **true** or **false**?

Examples of plain weave fabrics include polyester, cotton and calico. ....

10 Draw lines between the boxes to match each type of non-woven fabric to the correct description.

Needle felts		Adhesive, solvent or stitching joins the fibres together.
Wool felts		Sharp points are pushed through layers of fibres.
Bonded fabrics		The fibres are matted together using a solution.

11 How are yarns made? Tick the correct option.

    A Using a weaving loom. ◯

    B By spinning and twisting fibres together. ◯

    C By knitting in horizontal rows. ◯

    D By creating a series of interlocking loops. ◯

12 a) Briefly describe what a nanoparticle is.

b) Briefly describe what a nanotube is.

Modelling Colour and Decoration

Modelling

Modelling is an important part of design development because it allows you to **test and evaluate design ideas**.

Modelling can include producing...
- small **test pieces**
- **scale versions** of the end product
- full-size **prototypes**.

Small test pieces are best for **practising techniques** and **experimenting** with...
- **fabrics**
- **colours** and methods of application
- surface **decoration**
- techniques for **manipulating fabrics**.

Printing

Printing is used to **add colour and pattern** to fabrics.

Block printing...
- uses a wooden block with a design cut in **relief** (standing out) on it
- 'stamps' a design onto the fabric
- is suitable for any type of fabric.

Stencilling
- uses card with a design cut out of it
- involves colour being applied directly onto the fabric using a sponge or brush (colour will only appear in areas where the card is cut out).

Screen printing or silk-screen printing...
- uses a stencil under **a nylon screen** on a wooden frame
- involves dye being put on top of the screen and pushed through using a **squeegee**
- uses a different screen and stencil for each colour
- machinery uses the same principles.

Engraved roller printing...
- uses a series of **metal rollers** with a design **engraved** on them
- involves dye or pigment solution being pushed through a fine mesh on each roller
- produces a design where the size of the design is determined by the **circumference** of the roller
- uses a separate roller for each colour in the design
- can add designs to over 250m of fabric or wallpaper per minute.

Block Printing

Stencilling

Silk-Screen Printing

Printing (Cont.)

Heat transfer printing…
- uses a design **printed** onto **sublimation** paper
- transfers the design to fabric using **heated rollers**
- is only suitable for fabrics that have 50% or more synthetic content.

Computer transfer printing…
- uses an **image created** on a **computer** then printed onto transfer paper
- transfers the design by applying heat from an iron or heat press to the back of the paper.

Digital Printing…
- means that the **whole design and printing process** is carried out **by computer**
- can create complex designs quickly and easily
- is used in industry for sampling and to make **bespoke** (one-off) fabrics / garments.

A Digital Printer

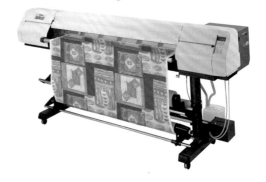

Dyeing

Dyeing is another common method of applying colour to fabrics. Fabric is immersed in a dye bath. The resulting **colours** depend on…
- the type of **fibre** (colours are stronger on natural fibres)
- the type of **dye**, i.e. synthetic or natural
- the type of **product** being dyed
- what **stage** of the production process colour is applied.

The following methods of dying can be used in the **classroom** or **industry**:

Pigment dyeing…
- uses a **binding agent** and **pigment** that are mixed and applied to the fabric
- is used in screen printing.

Natural / vegetable dyeing…
- uses colourings extracted from **natural products** like onion skins, beetroot and cochineal (beetle)
- uses a **mordant** (metallic oxide or salt **fixative**), which is needed to make the dye 'stick' to the fibres.

Industrial Practices　　　AQA • OCR

The following dying methods are **not suitable** for the classroom:

Direct dyeing…
- is a process that can only be done once and in a single colour
- does not involve a fixing process
- should not to be confused with using dyes, such as Dylon®.

Disperse dyeing…
- involves the fibre being placed in hot liquid and applying the dye under pressure
- is used for nylons, polyester and acrylics.

Modelling Colour and Decoration

Resist Methods of Dyeing
Edexcel • OCR

Resist methods of dyeing **stop the dye** penetrating certain areas of fabric to produce a pattern. Flour, rice paste, wax or string can all be used as 'resists'.

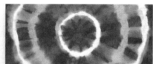

Wax	String
• Print blocks, brushes or specialist tools are used to apply hot molten wax to the surface of a fabric. • The fabric is dyed when the wax has cooled. • Additional colours can be added by removing some (but not all) of the wax using heat, e.g. from an iron. • **Batik** is a widely practised craft from Indonesia that uses wax as a resist – the wax is applied using a **tjanting**.	• String acts as a resist if it's tied around fabric tightly. • It's removed once the fabric has been dyed and dried. • Clear pattern lines are left where the ties were. • Pegs, bulldog clips and stitches can also be used for different effects.

Garment Dyeing
OCR

Garment dyeing involves dyeing garments **after they have been constructed**. It only works on fabrics with a natural or combined fibre content (where blended fibres or yarns have been used).

Surface Decoration

Adding **surface decoration** to fabrics or products can **enhance** appearance, add **texture** and create **interest**.

Appliqué…
- is **fabric shapes** sewn onto a **background fabric** using a fine zig-zag or straight stitch.
- often involves backing the fabric shapes with **interfacing** for strength
- can be used to develop simple or elaborate designs.

Patchwork…
- is small samples of **different fabrics sewn together**
- can be used to **combine textures** and create **different patterns**.

Embellishment…
- is **decorations** such as beads, buttons, shells and mirrors **attached** to a background fabric
- using **mirrors** for decoration is called '**Shisha**' work.

Surface Decoration (Cont.)

3D paints…
- are special paints that dry to leave a **raised design** on a fabric
- can be useful for **highlighting** specific areas of a 2D design.

Transfer printing techniques…
- use **disperse dyes** to create a design on paper
- **transfer** the design to fabric using heat from an iron / heat press
- use disperse dyes in powdered, liquid (transfer paints) or wax form
- can only be used on fabrics with **over 50% synthetic** content.

Transfers…
- are **images** that are **transferred** from special paper to fabric **using heat**
- can be created from **photos or computer generated images**
- are printed onto **special paper** using a standard printer
- use a range of papers for different weights and colours of fabric and different effects, e.g. glow-in-the-dark designs.

Embroidery…
- can be done by **hand or sewing machine**
- uses a wide variety of needles and threads
- involves decorative hand stitches, including cross stitch, herringbone stitch, satin stitch, French knots and chain stitch
- designs can be drawn onto water soluble fabric to provide a template. When the embroidery is complete, the fabric is washed and the template dissolves.

CAD embroidery…
- uses a specific type of sewing machine
- involves creating a design on the **machine** itself or on a **PC** using specific software (PC designs are **exported** to the sewing machine via a direct link or by using a special card).

Transfer Dyes

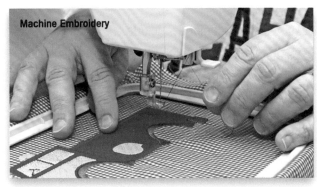
Machine Embroidery

Quick Test

1. Why is modelling important?
2. What type of printing process uses a squeegee?
3. What is a mordant?
4. Name one method of resist dyeing.
5. What printing method can print complex designs onto fabric quickly?

KEY WORDS

Make sure you understand these words before moving on!

- Modelling
- Prototypes
- Relief
- Sublimation
- Bespoke
- Pigment
- Mordant
- Resist
- Appliqué
- Embellishment
- Transfers

Modelling Fabrics

Fabrics

Designers must choose fabrics that have **properties** suitable for the functions of the end product.

Modelling allows you to practise working with these fabrics and experiment with different options and combinations.

Manipulation

Edexcel • OCR

Manipulating a yarn or fabric involves **changing its 'shape', structure or texture**. The process involves physical manipulation, e.g. bending, twisting or shaping, and sometimes heat and / or chemicals.

Manipulation techniques include...

- **felting** wool using soap and water to **mat the fibres** together
- using different stitches and seams to create a **3D appearance, e.g. pleats, tucks, gathering or darts**
- **twisting, plaiting or weaving** yarns or strips of fabrics
- **quilting** to create **surface texture**; sandwiching **wadding** or stuffing between layers of fabric and stitching through the layers
- **moulding** using heat and pressure to create tension in a fabric and mould if around a form
- stitching and folding fabrics and then using heat, such as steam, to set the shape, e.g. **Japanese 'Shibori'**.

Processes like Shibori work well with **synthetic fabrics** because they have **thermoplastic properties**, i.e. once heat is applied, the fabric will retain its shape unless the fabric is exposed to high temperatures again.

Felt

Pleats

Twisted Yarn

Quilting

Shibori

Combining Techniques

Combining methods of applying colour with surface decoration or manipulation can produce interesting effects.

Produce small test pieces to see if your ideas work before applying them to larger pieces of work.

Modelling with ICT

ICT can be very useful for modelling. You can use it to **evaluate and analyse** designs before you start modelling with fabrics, saving time and money.

Using computers to develop designs can be much quicker than traditional methods. Shapes, styles, colours, etc. can all be modified without having to start from the beginning each time.

Different software can be used to...

- **draft patterns**
- create **repeat patterns** from a single image
- view different **colourways** (colour variations and combinations)
- adjust the **scale** of designs to suit the product
- **present** ideas and designs in a professional way
- produce **3D representations**, using **image mapping**, of what the finished designs might look like.

Spreadsheets

Spreadsheet software (e.g. Microsoft Excel®) enables data to be organised in a grid. You can then carry out **calculations** using data in a specific range of cells.

Spreadsheets are useful for...

- **costing** / comparing products
- **analysing** fabrics or products
- costing / comparing different methods of production, e.g. batch or mass production.

Digital Cameras and Scanners

You can use a **digital camera** to take pictures of...
- things that inspire you
- similar products (to annotate for research)
- people using a product (to help develop or adapt your design)
- the different stages of development
- your end product for evaluation and analysis.

You can use a **scanner** to scan-in images and fabrics so that you can manipulate them using a CAD or graphics programme.

Quick Test

1. What can you use to felt wool?
2. How does quilting create surface texture?
3. What type of software is good for organising data so that calculations and analysis can be carried out?
4. Give two advantages of using ICT for modelling.
5. Name two ways in which ICT can be used in the modelling stage of textile design.

KEY WORDS

Make sure you understand these words before moving on!
- Manipulating
- Felting
- Colourways
- Image mapping
- Spreadsheet

Pattern Making

Patterns do not need to be created from scratch. There are different starting points that you can use.

Disassembly:

- Carefully **disassemble** (take apart) an existing product or garment.
- **Place** the pieces **on paper** and **pin** them in place.
- **Cut around** the pieces carefully.
- **Add pattern markings** and any amendments to your new paper pattern.

Commercial patterns:

- Available in packs from department stores and sewing shops.
- Pattern pieces are **graded** so you will need to cut out the size that is required.

Standard pattern block:

- **Pattern blocks** are **2D shapes** that make up different parts of a 3D garment.
- Come in **standard sizes** that are determined by the BSI (British Standards Institution).
- **Trace** around each block **on paper** before adjusting the size to fit, making adaptations and adding pattern markings.
- The method **used in industry**.

Pattern generation software:

- Select **parameters** and input **measurements** into the specialist software.
- Also provides a library of **standard patterns**.
- The pattern generated will contain all the pattern markings.

You must use standard pattern markings on all patterns.

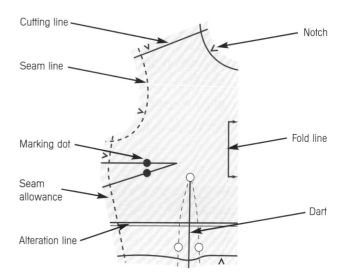

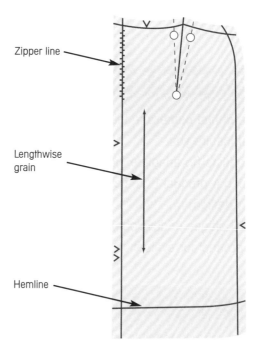

Lay Planning

The pattern needs to be arranged on the fabric so that there is as little waste as possible. This is called **lay planning**.

If the fabric has a **nap** or **pile**, like corduroy, the pattern pieces need to be arranged so that grain runs in the same direction, e.g. top to bottom. Fabrics with a bold pattern also need careful lay planning.

Toiles

A toile is a **prototype garment**. It's usually made from a **cheap fabric**, e.g. **calico**. The term is now used in general to refer to any model or prototype of a textile product. Several toiles may need to be made as adaptations are made to a design.

Toiles are very useful as they…
- **show how the product may look** when finished
- help to **identify modifications** to the pattern before production begins
- allow you to **estimate costs** depending on production methods
- help you to **evaluate** if the number of pattern pieces can be reduced to make manufacture less expensive.

You can use any of the methods described on page 60 to make a pattern for your toile. Alternatively you can make your own pattern.

Producing **small scale models** of your final piece can be useful, e.g. half scale (50%).

This is **cheaper** and allows you to…
- **test** design ideas
- **make changes** to the product
- estimate how much fabric may be needed for the final piece
- **practise** the skills needed to make the product.

Industrial Practices

In industry, **toiles** are created for all textile products and are an essential part of the design process.

Once the toile is made and the designer is happy with it, a sample garment can be made.

This process of making a toile allows the designer to **identify** the most **efficient methods and procedures** for manufacture.

Quick Test

1. How do commercial patterns cater for different sizes?
2. How do standard pattern blocks cater for different sizes?
3. What does 'disassembly' mean?
4. What is a toile?
5. Give two reasons for creating a toile.

KEY WORDS
Make sure you understand these words before moving on!
- Disassembly
- Pattern blocks
- Toile
- Prototype
- Lay planning
- Nap
- Pile
- Calico

Construction Techniques

Temporary Methods of Construction | OCR

Temporary methods of construction are used at various stages of modelling and making to **hold fabric in place** and **make adjustments**.

It's always best to use a temporary method before using a more permanent one to prevent costly mistakes!

Method	Description	
Pinning	• Holds sections of fabric in place.	
Tacking	• Long stitches sewn by hand. • Temporarily joins pieces of fabric together before stitching.	
Basting	• Loose hand sewn stitches. • Hold several layers of fabric in place before sewing.	
Tailors Tacking	• A loose, looped stitch. • Used to indicate or mark specific pattern lines. • Can be followed as a guide when using a sewing machine.	

Machine Stitching

Machine stitching is used for permanent joining and finishing. Many sewing machines come with a set of basic stitches:

- **Straight stitch (lockstitch)** – a basic straight stitch.
- **Single step zigzag** – a basic neatening stitch.
- **Double step zigzag** – for either finishing a seam or stitching jersey (knitted) fabrics together.
- **Chainstitch** – for stitching jersey (knitted) fabrics.
- **Overlock** – a combination of several stitches used for neatening the edge of a seam or garment.
- **Overlock with safety stitch** – combines an overlock with a chain or straight stitch so that seams can be stitched and finished at the same time.

Bonding and Welding
Edexcel

Bonding is a method of joining fabrics without stitching. A strip or sheet of adhesive web is placed between the two layers of fabric to be joined. Heat from an iron is then used to fuse them together.

In the textiles industry, **welding** is also used for joining fabrics. Welding uses **heat** or **radio frequency** (RF) to 'seal' the edges of fabrics like Gore-Tex® together.

Construction Techniques

Types of Seams

Plain seam:
- The **flattest seam** of all.
- Suitable for all fabric types.
- Seam edges need to be finished / neatened to stop fraying.

Double-stitched / flat-felled seam:
- **A self neatening** seam.
- Strong – used a lot on shirts, trousers, overalls and hardwearing garments.

French seam:
- For lightweight clothing, lingerie and children's wear.
- Best suited to lightweight fabrics, e.g. chiffon.
- Strong.
- **All edges are enclosed** (no finishing required).

Overlocked seam:
- Can be a 3, 4 or 5 thread overlocked seam.
- **Trims and neatens** the edge **whilst stitching** (must be used with care).
- Standard on many textile products made in industry.
- Requires an overlocker machine.
- Can be used inside a garment for neatness, or outside for decoration.

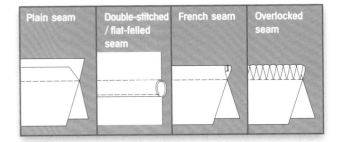

Plain seam	Double-stitched / flat-felled seam	French seam	Overlocked seam

Seam Finishes

Seam finishes are used to…
- give a neat, finished appearance
- prevent fraying.

All the examples below are used on a plain seam:

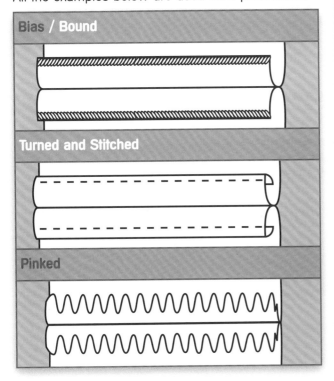

Bias / Bound

Turned and Stitched

Pinked

Quick Test

1. What temporary method would you use to hold a hem in place before machine stitching?
2. What type of machine stitch would you use to stitch and finish a seam at the same time?
3. What type of seam has the flattest finish?
4. What type of seam is best suited to lightweight fabrics?

KEY WORDS

Make sure you understand these words before moving on!
- Tacking
- Basting
- Bonding
- Welding
- Overlock
- Double stitch
- French seam
- Bias
- Pinked

Practice Questions

1 Which of the following processes is not an example of modelling? Tick the correct option.

    A Producing a scale prototype ⬭   **B** Producing small test pieces ⬭

    C Producing the final product ⬭   **D** Producing a toile ⬭

2 Which of the following statements about printing are true? Tick the correct options.

    A Sublimation paper is used for transfer printing. ⬭

    B All colours are applied using the same roller in engraved roller printing. ⬭

    C Digital printing can only be used to produce basic designs. ⬭

    D A squeegee is used to push dye through nylon when screen printing. ⬭

    E The design on a printing block is in relief. ⬭

    F Heat transfer printing is only suitable for natural fibres. ⬭

3 Draw line is between the boxes to match each term to the correct description.

Shisha	An ethnic type of embellishment using small mirrors.
Shibori	A prototype garment made of cheap fabric.
Appliqué	A Japanese technique for manipulating fabrics using steam.
Toile	Reinforced fabric shapes sewn onto fabric background.

4 Name two vegetables that can be used to dye textiles.

a) ....   **b)** ....

5 What term is used to describe dyeing techniques where the dye is prevented from penetrating certain areas of the fabric? Tick the correct option.

    A Disperse ⬭   **B** Resist ⬭

    C Mordant ⬭   **D** Direct ⬭

6 List five types of hand stitch used for decorative embroidery.

a) ....   **b)** ....

c) ....   **d)** ....

e) ....

7 What type of software is most appropriate for analysing production costs? Tick the correct option.

   A Publisher ⬭   **B** Spreadsheet ⬭

   C CAD ⬭   **D** Word Processing ⬭

8 Give two advantages of using CAD software for modelling textile products.

a) ....

b) ....

9 Who is responsible for setting the standard sizes for pattern blocks? Tick the correct option.

   A The designer ⬭   **B** The manufacturer ⬭

   C The British Standards Institution ⬭   **D** The Institute of Design and Technology ⬭

10 What type of fabric is usually used to make a toile? Tick the correct option.

   A Silk ⬭   **B** Wool ⬭

   C Nylon ⬭   **D** Calico ⬭

11 Match descriptions **A, B, C** and **D** with the types of stitch **1–4** in the table. Enter the appropriate number in the boxes provided.

   A A basic straight stitch. ⬭

   B A basic neatening stitch. ⬭

   C A combination of several stitches used to neaten edges. ⬭

   D Used for stitching knitted fabrics. ⬭

	Type of Stitch
1	Chain stitch
2	Lock stitch
3	Overlock
4	Single step zigzag

12 What type of temporary hand stitch can be used to create guides for when you use a sewing machine?

....

13 Give the name of the most appropriate type of seam for each of the following purposes.

a) A pair of jeans ....

b) A satin camisole top ....

c) Stitching and finishing the inside seam of a sweatshirt. ....

Quality Control

Quality Assurance and Quality Control

Quality assurance is a **guarantee of quality**. Businesses assure their customers that a product or service is of a high quality and fit for purpose. They produce documents outlining the systems used to ensure quality is maintained. Implementing the systems is the responsibility of everyone working in a business – it is called **Total Quality Management**. As in industry, you need to **check** the **quality** of your product…

- as it is being **designed**
- **during manufacture**
- at the **end of manufacture**.

Evaluating Designs

Evaluating your design at the development stage will help to ensure the end product…

- meets all the **criteria** in the initial brief and **design specification**
- is fit for **purpose**
- is suitable for your **target market**
- is **safe** to use and / or wear
- is **well made**.

It is a good idea to find out if the target market likes your ideas – show them some sketches and fabric samples and get some **feedback**.

At this stage, you can also carry out tests to help identify suitable materials (see facing page).

Only carry out **tests** if…

- they are **relevant**, i.e. they help you make decisions about the end product
- it is a **fair test**, i.e. different fabrics must be tested in exactly the same way under exactly the same conditions.

Identifying Quality Control Checks

Quality control (QC) checks are carried out during the manufacture of components and products to check…

- size
- appearance
- form
- colour
- flammability
- performance.

Your product and manufacturing specifications should contain details of when and how each QC check needs to be carried out.

The best time to **identify** what **QC checks** are needed is when you are **modelling / prototyping**. At this stage, a list of questions is sufficient, e.g.

- Are the seams secure?
- Is there needle damage?
- Are there missing stitches?
- Are the seams puckered or uneven?
- Are pocket and zips stitched correctly?
- Are components secured?

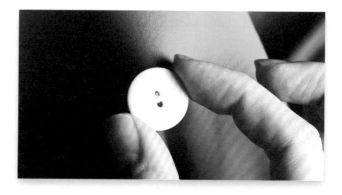

Technical Tests

Test	Description
Abrasion Sand paper Fabric Wooden block Tape Pin	• Pin or tape the fabric onto a flat board. • Rub the fabric with a sandpaper block in a backward and forward motion until a hole appears. • Record the number of rubs taken to create the hole.
Stretch (Elasticity) Bulldog clip Metal rod Fabric Weight Retort stand	• Set up a retort stand. • Hang a length of fabric (20cm x 10cm) from the top of the stand with a bulldog clip. • Add a 50g weight and leave the fabric for 24 hours. • Remove the weight and leave the fabric to relax for 10 minutes. • Measure the fabric to see how much extension has occurred.
Absorbency Pipette Fabric Embroidery hoop	• Write down the weight of a piece of fabric (15cm x 15cm). • Stretch the fabric onto an embroidery hoop. • Using coloured water and a pipette add droplets of water to the surface of the fabric. • Record what happens to the droplets, e.g. are they absorbed or do they remain on the surface? • When you have added 20 drops of water, weigh the fabric again. • Calculate the weight difference to find out how much water was absorbed.
Crease Recovery 	• Cut three equal samples of fabric (e.g. 10cm x 10cm). • Hold each piece in your hand for a different length of time (10, 20 and 30 seconds). • Record how the fabric reacts after each test (in writing or with a digital camera).
Insulation Thermometer Fabric wrapped around test tube Test tube (filled with water 100°C)	• Cover three test tubes with 'socks' made from the fabric being tested: Sock 1 is a single layer of fabric; Sock 2 is two layers of fabric stitched together; Sock 3 is two layers of fabric with a layer of wadding in between. • Fill each test tube with water heated to 100°C and place a thermometer in it. • Record the temperature in each test tube at regular time intervals. • Record the data in a spreadsheet and line graph.

Flammability
 	
Fabric sample
Bulldog clip
Retort stand
Metal rod Sand or water (for safety)
Fabric burning Taper to light fabric
	• Set up a retort stand.
	• Hang a length of fabric (20cm x 10cm) from the top of the stand over a bowl of water or sand.
	• Light the end of the fabric with a taper and observe the smell; smoke colour and density; time (i.e. how quickly the fabric takes to burn); behaviour, e.g. if the fabric drips when burning; appearance of fabric after burning.
	  – Cotton, linen and viscose smell like burning paper and turn into a grey powder.
	  – Wool and silk smell like burning hair, burn slowly and turn into cinder.
	  – Acetate burns quickly, drips and smells like vinegar.
	  – Polyester, nylon, acrylic, polypropylene and elastane all burn quickly, shrink, melt and drip.

Regulations and Standards

Regulations

Regulations are put in place to look after **consumer interests**, i.e. to ensure that products are of a good quality and safe to use.

Regulations are put in place by...

- **manufacturing groups**, to provide a code of practice for their members.
- the Government, through **Acts of Parliament**.

Standards

A standard is an agreed specification that sets out **precise criteria** to ensure the reliability and quality of a product or service.

Standards are regulated by the **British Standards Institution** (BSI). For Europe this is done by the **European Committee for Standardisation**.

Standards are **voluntary**. However, some laws and regulations refer to certain standards, making them **compulsory**.

Safety Standards

Textile products, and the components in them, have to achieve certain **safety standards** before they can be sold to the public. This means they have to pass a **rigorous** set of **tests**.

For example, under the BS 5867-1:2004 Specification for fabrics for curtains and drapes, fabrics must pass specific tests for...

- washing
- colour fastness (whether they fade)
- dry cleaning
- flammability
- dimensional stability (if they change length or width, during normal use, washing or cleaning)
- wear and tear.

Textiles must also conform to certain labelling requirements.

Manufacturers who meet BSI standards are awarded a Kitemark. The BSI Kitemark tells consumers that the product has been tested against nationally recognised standards. The Kitemark scheme is an independent and ongoing assessment process, that **ensures standards are achieved and maintained**.

The **Conformité Européenne 'CE' symbol** is the manufacturer's self-declaration that the product **meets the minimum requirements** from the EU directive to be allowed to be sold.

BSI Kitemark

'CE' Symbol

Regulations and Standards

Safety of Children's Products

Products for children have many factors that need to be considered, including the following:

- They must not have any parts or components that could come loose and **choke** or **harm** a child.
- They must not contain materials that could melt or catch fire.

- Dyes, paint and inks must not contain **harmful substances** or allergens.
- Fastenings must be **safe** and **easy to use**.

Legislation AQA

Here are just a few of the regulations that are applied to children's textile products:

- Nightwear Safety Regulations, 1985
- Nightwear Safety (Amendment) Regulations, 1987
- Children's Clothing Regulations, 1994
- The Toy Safety Regulations, 1995 (includes some clothing items, e.g. Bunny slippers)

- Food Imitation Regulations, 1989 (e.g. buttons mustn't resemble food)
- Code of Practice for the Design and Manufacture of Children's Clothing to Promote Mechanical Safety BS7907, 1997
- Children's Clothing (Hood Cord) Regulations, 1976

Safety of Other Products

Any product must be safe and easy for the **target market** to use. Below are some examples of health and safety considerations:

- Does the product need to withstand extreme temperatures, e.g. oven gloves, arctic clothing?
- Does the product need to provide protection from certain elements, e.g. tents, UV protective clothing, ski wear?

- Are there any specific user requirements, e.g. if your product is for elderly, are the fastenings easy for arthritic hands to use?
- Is the fabric strong and / or durable enough for its purpose, e.g. does the product need to hold anything with sharp edges, will it be used for carrying?

Quick Test

1. At what three stages should quality control checks be carried out?
2. Name two properties that can be tested scientifically.
3. Who is responsible for regulating standards in Britain?
4. Name one type of fabric that drips when it burns.
5. Give one example of an important safety consideration affecting children's products.

KEY WORDS

Make sure you understand these words before moving on!

- Fair test
- Flammability
- Abrasion
- Absorbency
- Insulation
- Standard
- Dimensional stability
- Kitemark

Health and Safety

Health and Safety in the Classroom

Safety is very important. In your classroom there will be **safety guidelines** that you will need to follow when using materials, components and equipment.

A **risk assessment** must always be carried out before making a product. That means...

- identifying the **equipment** and **processes** that are needed
- highlighting which equipment and processes are **potentially** hazardous
- putting a plan in place to remove or **reduce** each risk, including...
  - **safety procedures** for using equipment
  - **protective clothing** requirements.

Health and Safety in the Workplace

In industry, a Health and Safety Officer usually carries out a risk assessment and then follows these procedures:

- Creates a safety manual.
- Installs safety signs at key points, next to equipment.
- Creates a code of practice for all users of equipment.
- Outlines what safety wear needs to be used.
- Ensures that new and existing employees are fully trained on the equipment they will be using.

Safety procedures are controlled by Government Safety Laws, European Safety Laws, or other codes of practice such as...

- **Health and Safety at Work Act, 1974**
- **Workplace (Health, Safety and Welfare) Regulations, 1992**.

The **Control of Substances Hazardous to Health (COSHH)** Regulations, 2002, protect employees from the hazards of substances used in the work place through risk assessment.

Examples of Safety Signs

CAUTION
Dangerous chemical

DANGER 415 Volts

FLAMMABLE LIQUID

Eye protection must be worn

Potential Hazards

Process	Potential Hazards or Accidents	Safety Guidelines
Sewing	• Injuries to fingers and hands whilst cleaning or repairing • Eye injuries • Finger injuries from needles • Injuries from associated equipment	• Switch machine off when cleaning or repairing • Adjust eye guards • Keep fingers away from needles • Put equipment away eg. shears equipment or scissors after use
Spreading and cutting	• Finger or hand injuries from spreading and cutting machines • Finger or hand injuries from pressing mechanisms	• Add safety guards • Learn the correct way to handle the equipment
Fusing	• Finger and hand injuries in the press	• Check safety guidelines
Pressing	• Scalding from steaming equipment • Finger or hand injuries from pressing equipment	• Only turn on steam function when ready to use the steam • Operators must be well trained in the use of the machine before use
Stain removal	• Breathing in solvent vapours	• Rooms where solvents are used must be well ventilated
General working area	• Tripping or falling • Electrical injury • Incorrect handling of materials • Incorrect lifting	• Work area to be kept clean and tidy • Never use a machine with damaged covers • Don't carry too many things at once • Learn the correct way to lift
Dyeing or printing equipment	• Inhalation of dye dust • Inhalation of dye vapours • Staining of skin with dyes	• Wear appropriate mask and eye cover • Ensure correct ventilation • Wear protective aprons and gloves

Quick Test

1. Name two ways of reducing risks.
2. List three potential hazards of sewing.
3. Give three general safety guidelines that apply to the classroom and the workplace.
4. What does COSHH stand for?

KEY WORDS

Make sure you understand these words before moving on!
• Risk assessment
• Hazardous

Practice Questions

1. Which of the following factors are checked during manufacture using quality control checks? Tick the correct options.

   A Appearance ◯   **B** Quantity ◯

   C Design ◯   **D** Size ◯

   E Flammability ◯   **F** Purpose ◯

   G Performance ◯

2. The following statements describe the different stages in a standard textiles test for stretch or elasticity. Number them **1– 5** to show the correct order of events.

   A Remove the weight and leave the fabric to 'relax' for 10 minutes. ◯

   B Hang a 50g weight from the end of the fabric and leave for 24 hours. ◯

   C Set up a retort stand. ◯

   D Measure the length of the fabric ◯

   E Hang a strip of fabric of a known length from the top of the stand. ◯

3. Choose the correct word from the options given to compare the following sentences.

conditions	fair	method	property

   If you are testing the same .... in different fabrics, you must make sure that you

   use exactly the same .... for each fabric and that they are all tested under the

   same .... to ensure that it is a .... test.

4. **a)** Which organisation is responsible for controlling the standards that are applied to products in Britain?

   ....

   b) How do consumers know if a product has achieved the relevant standards?

   ....

5. All the materials and components used to make children's products must pass rigorous safety tests. Suggest one thing that the following items might be tested for.

   a) Fabric

   ....

   b) Components

   ....

6 Which of the following are sensible ways of reducing the risk associated with using machinery? Tick the correct options.

    A Follow the safety procedures for operating the machine carefully. ◯

    B Pay attention to any safety signs on display. ◯

    C Play around with the machine until you understand how to use it. ◯

    D Wear the correct protective clothing, e.g. gloves or safety goggles. ◯

    E Avoid using any processes that require special machinery. ◯

7 Draw lines between the boxes to match each fabric to the behaviour it displays when burned.

Nylon		Smells like burning paper and turns into grey powder.
Cotton		Burns quickly, shrinks, melts and drips.
Acetate		Burns slowly and smells like burning hair.
Wool		Burns quickly and smells like vinegar.

8 For each process listed below, give one potential hazard and an appropriate safety measure.

    a) Pattern cutting

      Hazard: ....

      Safety Measure: ....

    b) Sewing

      Hazard: ....

      Safety Measure: ....

    c) Pressing

      Hazard: ....

      Safety Measure: ....

    d) Dyeing

      Hazard: ....

      Safety Measure: ....

Planning Production

Manufacturing Specification

A **manufacturing specification** (production plan) must provide a **clear set of instructions and diagrams** to enable the manufacturer to make the product exactly as the designer envisaged (see p.33).

It is important that it includes...
- a **time line** and plan for each stage of manufacture
- details of necessary **quality control checks**.

Gantt Charts and Time Plans   AQA • OCR

A **Gantt chart** shows...
- the **overall timeline** for a project
- the **separate stages** / tasks that need to be completed
- the **time allocated** for each stage
- the **order of work**.

They can also be used to compare estimated and actual timings.

In industry, time plans like this must be accurate as they are used to calculate...
- the **overall cost** of the product
- the **cost of each process** used to make and finish the product
- **how long** it will take to complete a customer order.

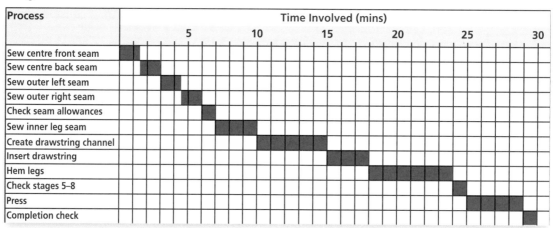

Process	Time Involved (mins)
	5 10 15 20 25 30
Sew centre front seam	
Sew centre back seam	
Sew outer left seam	
Sew outer right seam	
Check seam allowances	
Sew inner leg seam	
Create drawstring channel	
Insert drawstring	
Hem legs	
Check stages 5–8	
Press	
Completion check	

Quality Control Checks

Details of **quality control checks** should include...
- **when** the check is to take place
- **what** is to be checked
- **how** it is to be checked
- what the **tolerances** are.

A tolerance is **a range of acceptable measurements**. Anything outside this range is classed as faulty.

For example, a seam may need to be 3mm from the edge of a pocket but, if there is a tolerance of + / - 1mm, any seam between 2mm and 4mm from the edge is acceptable.

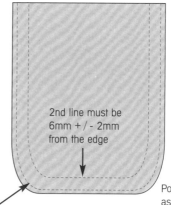

2nd line must be 6mm + / - 2mm from the edge

1st line must be 3mm from the edge + / - 1mm

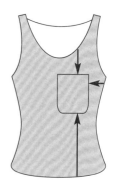

Pocket must be placed exactly as sample. Allowed 2–3mm tolerance, this space is crucial as needed for heat transfer placement print.

Systems and Control

Manufacturing activities must be carried out in a specific order, otherwise there will be chaos. **Systems** are put in place to ensure that procedures and processes are carried out in an **organised** way.

Control systems are put in place to ensure everything **goes to plan**. They are often represented as flow charts with three main areas:

- **Inputs** – the **starting point** for the whole process, e.g. the materials to be used.
- **Transformation processes** – processes that **change the inputs**, e.g. pattern cutting, assembly and finishing.
- **Outputs** – **the outcome** of the process, e.g. the finished garment.

Feedback is a built-in method of **correcting problems** that occur within a system. At several points during the production process, **checks** are carried out on the product. If the checks reveal a fault, it is reported back to the appropriate stage so the fault can be corrected.

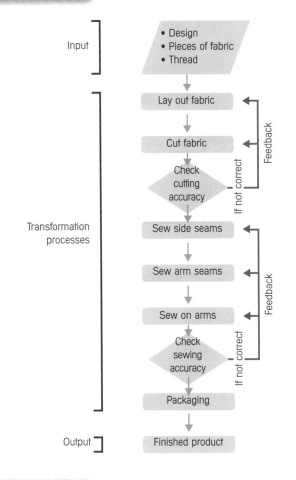

Commercial Manufacturing

Before manufacture, the space within a factory needs to be organised so that…

- all the different inputs, processes and outputs are allocated an appropriate work space
- work 'flows' from one stage to the next.

Quick Test

1. **True** or **false**: In industry, time plans are used to estimate the cost of a product.
2. What is a tolerance?
3. Name two things that a Gantt chart shows?
4. What affect does a transformation process have on an input?
5. What is it called when faults are reported back during the production process?

KEY WORDS
Make sure you understand these words before moving on!
- Gantt chart
- Tolerances
- Inputs
- Transformation processes
- Outputs
- Feedback

Planning Production

The diagram below shows how a product is made in a factory. The movement of the product from one area of the factory to another, as each process is completed, is indicated by arrows.

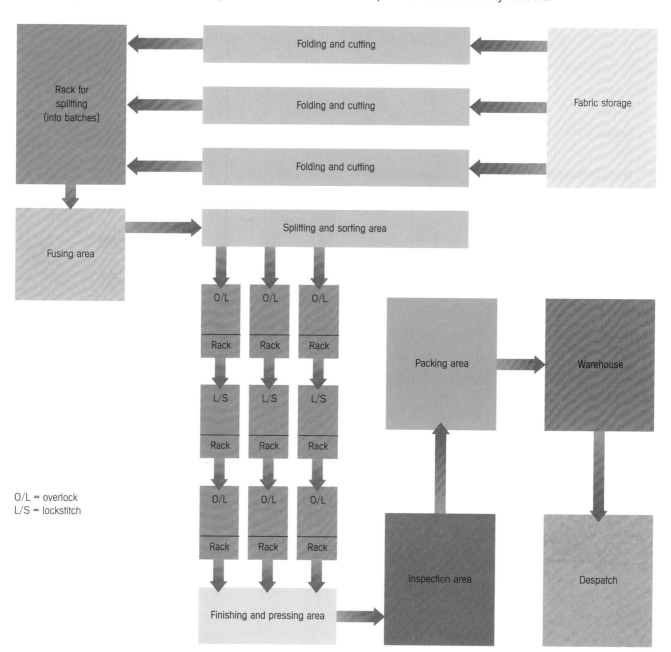

O/L = overlock
L/S = lockstitch

Control Checks

Quantity control checks take place in...

- fabric storage
- the splitting phases
- the packing area, warehouse and dispatch.

Quality control checks take place...

- in fabric storage
- after each fusing and sewing phase
- in the finishing, inspection and packing areas.

Computers in the Textiles Industry

Computer Systems

In industry, the key **advantages** of using **computers** are that they…

- provide an effective means of **presentation**
- **reduce** the **time** taken to create products
- **improve communication**
- **reduce repetitive work**
- **decrease costs** and **increase efficiency**.

Examples of computers systems used in the textile industry include…

- **Computer Aided Administration (CAA)** – computers are used for marketing, sales order processing and stock control
- **Computer Aided Design (CAD)** – computers are used for developing designs, pattern making, pattern grading, marker production and lay planning
- **Computer Aided Manufacture (CAM)** – computers are used for store design, lay planning and cutting, sewing and pressing
- **Computer Integrated Manufacture (CIM)** – a system that uses computers at every stage of planning, design and manufacture
- **Electronic Point of Sale (EPOS)** – a computerised system that speeds up sales transactions and monitors stock levels.

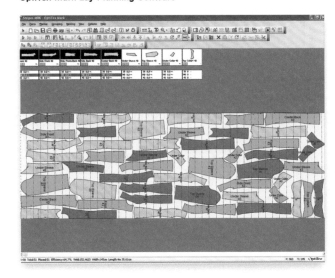

OptiTex Mark Lay Planning Software

New Technology

Many companies take advantage of new technologies, such as…

- Skype
- instant messaging
- video conferencing
- blogging
- E-retail
- Interactive design
- Networking sites, e.g. Bebo, My Space and You Tube
- virtual imaging.

Virtual imaging can be used to show what a design will look like before it's manufactured, for example…

- fashion designers may use software like 3D Runway Designer to display their designs on **virtual models**
- interior designers may use mapping software or specialist programs to create **virtual interiors**.

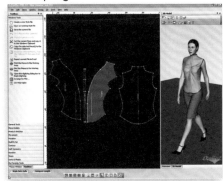

Created using 3D Runway Designer from OptiTex Ltd (www.optitex.com)

Computers in the Textiles Industry

Below are examples of how computers and other pieces of digital equipment may be used at the various stages of design and manufacture:

Stage	Purpose	Examples
Research and Presenting	• Collecting and recording information • Relaying digital imagery	• Internet and email (including on-line trend services) • Digital camera • Graphics software • Word processing software • Video conferencing
Design	• Creating and developing visual designs • Developing specification sheets • Experimenting with colourways • Developing prototypes	• Graphics software • Specialised textiles software • Scanner • Digital camera • Graphics tablet • Digital printer • PDM software • CAD Systems
Manufacturing / Production	• Making patterns • Making the end products • Controlling machinery • Production costing	• Lay planning / cutting tables • Digitisers • 3D body scanning equipment • Computerised sewing / knitting / weaving machines • Digital printing equipment • EDI (Electronic Data Interchange)
Distribution	• Stock control and dispatch • Order processing	• Tagging (RFID) • Word processing / Database software • Spreadsheet software • Stock / asset management software
Sales	• Promoting the product, e.g. advertising • Sales channels, e.g. website / E-tailing • E-Commerce • Security tagging	• Graphics software • Word processing software • Digital printer • Digital camera • EPOS software • PDM software

Computers in the Textiles Industry

The Three Phases

There are **three phases** to the creation of a **commercial textiles** product:

- Pre-production (the design phase)
- Production
- Post-production.

ICT is used in all of these phases:

Pre-production

- **Research** ideas on-line.
- **Present** ideas using mood boards developed in specialist graphics packages.
- **Develop** initial designs using vector drawing graphics software.
- **Design** fabric range using specialised CAD graphics software.
- **Model** fabric on product using 2D mapping or 3D Image Draping system.
- Garment **specification** created.

Production Phase

- Product **testing** on all relevant parts.
- 3D image can be generated via a flat 2D pattern and mapped on a computer model called an '**avatar**'.
- **Costings** are generated using PDM (Product Data Management) software and Manufacturing Specifications.
- PDM systems are used for **tracking** materials and components for the product before manufacture starts.
- Product specification is used with specialist software for **pattern making**.
- A **lay plan** is created, using software which calculates the best way of laying all the pattern pieces on the fabrics to minimise wastage.
- Fabrics are cut out using a specialised **cutting** table.
- **Production sample** is made.
- Product sent to **production line** (which may be in a manufacturing plant abroad).
- **Product is made**.

Post-production Phase

- **Sales and Marketing** Department use a virtual design system, which shows how the product can be displayed on in-store systems.
- To **launch the product** it can be placed on the web and a virtual fashion show can take place.
- Product is sent to **retail outlet** where it can be tracked with EPOS (a computerised barcode system).
- **On-line retailing**.

Quick Test

1. Give two key advantages of using computers in the textiles industry.
2. List three new technologies that could be used in industry.
3. Name two pieces of ICT equipment, other than a computer, that can be used at the design stage.
4. What are the three phases of commercial manufacture?

KEY WORDS

Make sure you understand these words before moving on!

- Computer Aided Manufacture (CAM)
- Computer Aided Design (CAD)
- Avatar
- Lay plan

Industrial Clothing Manufacture

Production Systems

The **four** main **types of production** system are...

- **Haute Couture**
- **individual or job production**
- **batch production**
- **mass production**.

The system used depends on the...

- type of **product**
- **number of products** to be made
- **number of components and processes** used
- quantity **required** for each delivery.

Type	Description	Example
Individual or Job Production	<ul><li>Also known as '**Making Through**'.</li><li>The product is made by an **individual** or small team from start to finish.</li><li>**Traditional methods** of manufacture are used.</li><li>The operators are **highly skilled** and use versatile equipment.</li><li>**Haute Couture** is an extreme example of this production method.</li></ul>	
Batch Production	<ul><li>A **reasonable number** of products are produced, possibly to meet **seasonal demand**, e.g. swimwear.</li><li>Production **costs** are considerably **less** than for individual production.</li></ul>	
Mass Production	<ul><li>Used to manufacture **large numbers** of **identical products** over a **long period** of time.</li><li>Products are usually **not complicated** and can be made **cheaply**, e.g. tights or vest top.</li></ul> Types of mass production include... <ul><li>**synchronised / straight-line production** – work is passed along a **production line** where each operator is responsible for one task, which they perform repeatedly.</li><li>**repetitive flow production** – manufacture is divided into **sub-assembly lines** that each focus on one area of the process.</li><li>**continual flow production** – used for massive volume items; the process runs **24 hours a day** and is never shut down.</li></ul>	

Industrial Clothing Manufacture

Other Production Systems

Cell production or section systems…
- divide the workforce into small teams that all produce the same product
- rely on each team to take responsibility for the quality of the products produced by them.

Progressive Bundle Production…
- uses small teams that are each responsible for a particular part of the production process
- is like cell production, but for individual parts of the garment.

'Off-the-Peg' Manufacture

Except for Haute Couture and individual / job production, the different production systems are designed to produce '**off-the-peg**' garments (ready-made garments in standard sizes).

Using templates in standard sizes helps to keep costs down.

One-off garments that are made to specific measurements for an individual are called '**bespoke**' and are usually far more expensive.

Just-in-Time Stock Control

Just-in-time stock management means that materials, components and sub-assemblies are **delivered a short time before they are needed**. This means that…
- less space is required for storage
- no money is wasted on surplus stock.

With this type of stock control there must be no mistakes, otherwise production can be held up.

Quick Test

1. Name a textile product that can be mass produced.
2. What is synchronised production?
3. Give an example of a textile product that is batch produced.
4. What is the difference between an off-the-peg garment and a bespoke garment?
5. Give one advantage of just-in-time stock management.

KEY WORDS
Make sure you understand these words before moving on!
- Haute Couture
- Job production
- Batch production
- Mass production
- Synchronised production
- Production line
- Off-the-peg
- Bespoke
- Just-in-time

Practice Questions

1 What do the following abbreviations stand for?

a) CIM ....

b) CAA ....

c) CAD ....

d) CAM ....

2 Draw a line between the boxes to match each ICT tool to the correct stage of production.

Sales	RFID Tagging.
Distribution	EPOS and PDM software.
Manufacturing and Production	Graphics tablet.
Design	Lay planning software and computerised cutting tables.

3 **a)** What type of production is continuous and produces a large volume of identical products? Tick the correct option.

A Batch production ⬭   **B** Job production ⬭

C Mass production ⬭   **D** Haute Couture ⬭

b) What type of production method is best suited to seasonal products, where fairly large numbers are sold for a limited period each year? Tick the correct option.

A Batch production ⬭   **B** Job production ⬭

C Mass production ⬭   **D** Haute Couture ⬭

c) What type of production method is the cheapest to operate? Tick the correct option.

A Batch production ⬭   **B** Job production ⬭

C Mass production ⬭   **D** Haute Couture ⬭

4 Fill in the missing words to complete the following sentences.

a) .... are put in place to ensure that events happen

according to plan. They are often represented by .... charts.

b) .... are the factors which act as the starting point for the whole process.

5 Which of the following occur during the Post-production Phase? Tick correct options.

A Product testing ◯

B Presenting ideas ◯

C Product launch ◯

D Pattern making ◯

E Research and intelligence gathering ◯

F Tracking of product with EPOS ◯

G Tracking of materials with PDM software ◯

6 What term is used to describe processes that change an input in some way? Tick the correct option.

A Control ◯   B Transformation ◯

C Synchronized ◯   D Output ◯

7 What is the name given to the type of chart shown below? _____

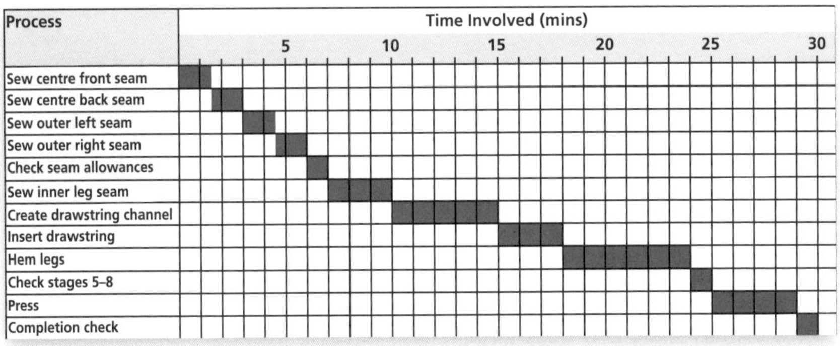

Process	Time Involved (mins)						
		5	10	15	20	25	30
Sew centre front seam							
Sew centre back seam							
Sew outer left seam							
Sew outer right seam							
Check seam allowances							
Sew inner leg seam							
Create drawstring channel							
Insert drawstring							
Hem legs							
Check stages 5–8							
Press							
Completion check							

8 Match the descriptions **A-D** to the manufacturing terms **1-4**. Write the correct number in the box provided.

	Terms
1	Just-in-time
2	Off-the-peg
3	Bespoke
4	Making through

A An alternative term for describing individual or job production methods. ◯

B A method of stock control that relies on materials being delivered shortly before manufacture. ◯

C Garments that are produced in multiple quantities and in standard sizes. ◯

D Custom-made garments and products. ◯

Advertising and Marketing

Advertising

Advertising is any type of **media** that **informs** and / or **influences** consumers about products.

It is used to…
- **create product awareness**
- launch new products
- get customers to upgrade to a newer / better product.

Some of the media that are used by advertisers are…
- television, radio and cinema
- magazines
- national and local newspapers
- trade magazines
- specialist websites
- workers' uniforms, e.g. logos.

In shops, further advertising is used:
- Posters
- **Point-of-sale** material
- **Swing tickets**
- Packaging
- Information booklets
- Shop displays.

All advertising is **controlled** by **legislation** (laws) put in place by bodies like the **Advertising Standards Authority** to **protect** the public from misleading adverts, for example…
- The British Code of Advertising
- The Fair Trading Act
- The Independent Broadcasting Act.

Marketing

When textiles products are ready for **marketing** (the process of promoting, advertising and selling a product) they are taken to a distribution centre. From the distribution they are sent to…

- **Wholesalers**
- Retail outlets, e.g. shops and concessions
- **Mail order** catalogues
- **E-retailers**, i.e. companies that sell products via the Internet.

E-Commerce

E-Commerce is a term used to describe **electronic buying and selling**, e.g. via the Internet and mobile phones / text messages.

Alternative terms include, E-Tailing, On-line trading or Internet shopping.

When you buy goods using E-commerce, you have the **same rights** as when you buy from a shop or by distance sale (e.g. mail order) anywhere in the UK and EU. Other rules and regulations apply to countries outside the EU.

The Purpose of Packaging

Packaging is used to...
- **protect** products during transport
- provide **information**
- **promote** the product.

The packaging that is used for textiles products comes in two categories:
- **Primary packaging** – the packaging that the product is sold in; can consist of several layers, e.g. a box and cellophane wrapper.
- **Secondary packaging** – used to **transport** multiple products, e.g. cartons, pallets and shrink wrap.

Packaging Designs   OCR

A designer will produce the **primary packaging** for a product. It will have its own **design specification**, which will take into account...
- what the **product** is
- the **values** of the product, e.g. polythene would not be suitable for packaging organic products
- the **target market** for the product
- how much **protection** is needed
- whether the package needs to be **transparent** / have a window
- whether the customer needs to be able to take the product from the package to **test it** / **try it on**

- other **specific criteria**, e.g. it needs to be lightweight and easy to carry.

As packaging is usually **discarded** after use, it is important to consider how its impact on the **environment** can be reduced, for example...
- can recycled / sustainable materials be used to make it?
- can it be recycled?

Some ways in which companies address these issues include...
- limiting the layers of packaging
- using **biodegradable** materials.

Quick Test

1. Name two types of advertising used in shops.
2. What is E-Commerce?
3. What is the difference between primary and secondary packaging?
4. Name one way in which the impact of packaging on the environment can be reduced.
5. List three important considerations when designing primary packaging.

KEY WORDS
Make sure you understand these words before moving on!
- Media
- Point-of-sale
- Swing ticket
- Legislation
- Marketing
- Wholesalers
- Mail order
- E-retailers
- E-Commerce
- Primary packaging
- Secondary packaging

Labelling

Labelling

Textiles **labels** provide information, which is **controlled by legislation**. A typical textiles label will include...

- **fibre content** – in descending order (the fibre with the highest content first)
- **chemical names** of materials used; not just trade names
- **standard number(s)** – to show which standard(s) the product meets
- **country of origin**
- **product details**, e.g. type, size and style
- **safety advice**, e.g. keep away from fire
- **care instructions**.

Other things found on labels include...

- the retailer's symbol or **logo** (promotional material)
- the retailer's **store and product number** (for tracking the product)
- a **barcode** (a code made up of lines and numbers that provides product information, e.g. manufacturer and price)
- **ethical information**, e.g. whether the product is organic or tested on animals.

There are different types of label:

- **permanent** – stitched onto the garment; contains **legally required** information, e.g. fibre content
- **swing tickets** – attached to the product; often contains size, style and price information
- **gummed** – usually found on the outside of product or on its packaging.

Permanent Label

Swing Ticket

Aftercare Labels

Aftercare labels tell you how best to clean and care for a product. This is sometimes called **product maintenance** or **washcare**.

Machine wash	Hand wash	Dry clean	Iron or press
⌷40	🖐	Ⓟ	⊿

Consumer Protection   AQA • OCR

Some of the **key regulations** that apply to clothing and textiles labelling are…

- **The Trade Descriptions Act** – it's illegal to make false claims about a product
- **The Sale of Goods Act** – products must match their description, be of a satisfactory quality and be fit for purpose

- **The Weights and Measures Act** – it's illegal to sell products that are short-measured, i.e. weigh less than the amount on the label
- **The Textiles Products (Indication of Fibre Content) Regulations** – it's a legal requirement to state the fibre content of a fabric on a label, in descending order using chemical names.

Flammability   AQA • OCR

It's **illegal** to label products as '**non-flammable**' or '**flame-resistant**' unless they have met the strict **standard for low flammability** set by the British Standards Institution.

Special labelling regulations apply to childrens' nightwear and upholstered furniture:

- **Children's nightwear** must be made from materials that have met the standard for **low flammability**. They must also carry a warning to stay away from fire and / or naked flames.
- All **upholstered furniture** must carry a fire label of some sort. It should either say '**resistant**' (if made from flame-proofed material) or carry a warning label about the dangers of fire from cigarettes and / or flames.

Quick Test

1. What are the three types of label commonly used on textiles products?
2. Which type of label is used for legally required information?
3. In what order should fibres be listed on a label?
4. What warning must be included on children's nightwear?
5. What is the Trade Descriptions Act?

KEY WORDS
Make sure you understand these words before moving on!
- Fibre content
- Barcode
- Aftercare
- The Trade Descriptions Act

Practice Questions

1 a) List three examples of advertising media.

    i) ....   **ii)** ....

    iii) ....

b) List three types of advertising used in shops.

    i) ....   **ii)** ....

    iii) ....

2 What is advertising legislation? Tick the correct option.

    A Advice to advertisers ◯   **B** Advertising materials ◯

    C Laws controlling advertising ◯   **D** A company's advertising policy ◯

3 List three different marketing channels for textiles products.

    a) ....   **b)** ....   **c)** ....

4 Write **Primary** or **Secondary**, as appropriate, alongside each of the following examples of packaging.

    a) A large, brown, corrugated cardboard carton ....

    b) A colourful laminated box with a transparent window ....

    c) A wooden palette ....

    d) A thin cellophane wrapper with stickers on it ....

5 a) Briefly describe how fibre content should be given on a label for a textiles product.

....

....

b) What type of label is used to give fibre content? Tick the correct option.

    A Permanent ◯

    B Swing ticket ◯

    C Gummed label (applied by manufacturer) ◯

    D Gummed label (applied by retailer) ◯

c) In addition to fibre content, what other pieces of information are found on the label of a textiles product as standard? Tick the correct options.

A   Care instructions ◯

B   Type of dye used ◯

C   Size ◯

D   Country of origin ◯

E   Year of manufacture ◯

F   Designer's name ◯

G   Chemical names of fibres ◯

6 What do the following symbols mean?

a) ⌷40⌷ ....

b) Ⓟ ....

7 Draw lines between the boxes to match each regulation to the correct description.

| The Textiles Products Regulations |

| The fibre content of a fabric must be stated on a label. |

| The Trade Descriptions Act |

| Products must match their description, be fit for purpose and of satisfactory quality. |

| The Weights and Measures Act |

| A company must not make claims about their products that are not true. |

| The Sale of Goods Act |

| It is illegal to sell products that weigh less than the amount stated on the label. |

8 What two types of textiles products must include information about flammability on their labels?

a) ....   **b)** ....

9 Give an example of a piece of ethical information that a manufacturer might want to include on the label of one of their products.

....

Answers

Quick Test Answers

Page 7

1. **Accept any three of the following:** to provide protection; to provide comfort; for decoration; to make practical tools.
2. **Accept any two of the following:** roads and infrastructure; civil engineering; transport; flooring; medicine; agriculture; architecture; specialised protective clothing.
3. Wax.
4. A squeegee.
5. **Accept any one of the following:** joining; finishing hems, seams and / or fabrics; decorative edging.
6. To cut fabric without causing fraying.
7. Any item that is incorporated into the finished product.

Page 11

1. Primary and secondary research.
2. Taking a product apart to get a better understanding of how it works and how it was made.
3. **Accept any one of the following:** to find out how products are used by consumers; to get feedback on designs and prototypes; to observe people using products; to consider the ergonomics and anthropometrics of a product.
4. **Accept any three of the following:** art; photographs; materials and fabrics; exhibitions, fairs and shows; cinema; travel; architecture; furniture and interior design; **any other sensible answer**.
5. To produce reliable and helpful results.

Page 15

1. Mixing white with a colour gives a tint; mixing black with a colour gives a shade.
2. A colour scheme featuring a single colour (can include different shades, tones and tints).
3. Complementary colours appear opposite each other on the colour wheel and produce a contrast.

4. The essential criteria and the desirable criteria for the design.
5. After final modifications have been made to the prototype.

Answers to Practice Questions

Pages 16–17

1. 'Textiles' is a general term used to describe any product that is made from fabric.
2. a) **Accept any two of the following:** batik pots; screen printing equipment; fabric paints and / or crayons; **any other sensible answer**.
   b) **In any order:** iron; heat press.
   c) **In any order:** sewing machine; overlocker.
3. a)–c) **Accept any three of the following:** computerised sewing machine; knitting machine; weaving loom; **any other sensible answer**.
4. a)–c) **Accept any three of the following:** surveys and / or questionnaires; focus groups; visiting shows and / or exhibitions; **accept any other sensible answer**.
5. Primary research is carried out by you; secondary research has been carried out by somebody else.
6. disassembly; identify; new; existing.
7. A, C and G.
8. Primary – Can't be mixed from any other colours.
   Secondary – Mixed from two primary colours.
   Tertiary – Mixed from three primary colours in different amounts.
9. C.
10. a) **Accept any sensible answer, e.g.** high-visibility vests, children's toys.
    b) **Accept any sensible answer, e.g.** camouflaged army uniforms.
    c) **Accept any sensible answer, e.g.** bedding, baby clothes.

Quick Test Answers

Page 19

1. At every stage of the product's life cycle energy and resources are used and waste is produced.
2. Dyeing and finishing.
3. The raw materials that were used to make the product are being wasted.
4. They require cleaning and maintenance through processes like washing, dry-cleaning and ironing, which use energy and produce waste.
5. It generates a large amount of unnecessary waste (because products that are still functional are discarded when they go out of fashion).

Page 23

1. **Accept any one of the following:** stuffing for bedding / car seats; industrial felt; **any other sensible answer**.
2. **Accept any two of the following:** charity shop; clothing bank at supermarket / recycling centre; **any other sensible answer**.
3. Polyester fleeces / duvets.
4. Forestry Stewardship Council.
5. Harmful substances.
6. 3

Answers to Practice Questions

Page 24–25

1. large; manufacturing; aftercare; waste; (In any order:) energy and resources.
2. **Accept any one of the following:** resins can be used to stop fabrics shrinking; softeners can be used to improve the 'feel' of the fabric; **any other sensible answer**.
3. The dyeing process uses energy, produces chemical waste, and uses and contaminates large volumes of water. Double dyeing means that twice the amount of energy and water is used and twice the amount of waste and contamination is produced.
4. a)–b) **In any order:** use natural dyes; use cold water dyes; **any other sensible answer**.
5. a)–b) **In any order:** used in the automotive industry (to stuff seats, etc.); used to make emergency relief blankets; incorporated into new fabrics; **any other sensible answer**.
6. The process by which new designs, trends and fashions make old designs obsolete despite the fact that they're still functional and effective.
7. C.
8. B, C, F and G.

Answers

Environmental Factors (Cont.)

9. Primary recycling – The product is reusable in its existing state.
    Secondary recycling – Also called physical recycling; the materials are shredded or melted before being reused.
    Tertiary recycling – Also called chemical recycling; the materials are broken down and reformulated.

10. **a)–c) In any order:** charity shop; clothing / textiles banks; use the materials to make new products; **any other sensible answer**.
11. A, D, E and F.

Designing

Quick Test Answers
Page 27
1. False.
2. Future trends.
3. **Accept any three of the following:** lifestyle; popular culture; new fibres and materials; technological developments; other fields of design; **any other sensible answer**.
4. Because they have to start designing products two or three years in advance.

Page 31
1. **Accept any two of the following:** fabric crayons; transfer crayons; printing; dyeing; stencilling; **any other sensible answer**.
2. Texture.
3. **Accept any one of the following:** modelling; scale products; test pieces; **any other sensible answer**.
4. To be able to select the best fabric for the job.
5. Front, back and (where appropriate) side views.

Page 33
1. Before making a prototype product.
2. **Accept any three of the following:** list of materials / components; list of tools and equipment; flowchart / plan of work; timelines for each stage; QC checks; details of critical points; possible problems and solutions; correct pattern annotation.
3. So that the manufacturer can make the product exactly as the designer envisaged it.

Answers to Practice Questions
Page 34–35
1. **a)–b) In any order:** to record ideas; to collect information.
2. C
3. Trend boards are similar to mood boards but focus on future trends rather than current trends.
4. B and D.
5. Something decorative that is added to enhance a design (e.g. embroidery, lamination, adding sequins, beads and ribbons).
6. **a)** Ergonomic **b)** Anthropometric.
7. C.
8. Proportion – Experimenting with the size / scale of the design or different elements within the design.
    Development – Involves refining an idea to make it better, or to make the product easier to use.
    Product specification – It contains all the instructions and information needed to produce a prototype of the product.
9. **a)–d) Accept any four of the following:** front and back views; measurement details; exploded drawings; details of seams; annotations highlighting key details; **any other sensible answer**.
10. B.
11. B, D and E.
12. The tactile characteristics or 'feel' of a fabric.

Materials and Components

Quick Test Answers
Page 39
1. Natural fibres are naturally occurring; synthetic fibres are man-made.
2. True.
3. Knitted fabrics are more elastic because they're made from interlocking loops of yarn.
4. Plain weave.
5. To bond fibres.

Page 41
1. Rubber / latex.
2. **Accept any two of the following:** waterproof; UV protection; maintain body temperature.
3. The fabric will have the combined properties of the different fibres.

Page 43
1. **Accept any two of the following:** wool; silk; viscose.
2. **Accept any two of the following:** Cotton; linen; viscose; rayon.
3. Wool.
4. Kevlar and biosteel.
5. It is insulating / heat and flame resistant.

Page 47
1. Enzymes.
2. It gives the fabric a smooth finish.
3. Wool.
4. A silicon-based chemical is sprayed on the fabric.
5. Advantage: removes natural colour. Disadvantage: Weakens the fabric / uses strong chemicals.

Page 51
1. Change colour at different temperatures.
2. **Accept any two of the following:** carbon; steel; nickel; silver.
3. **Accept any three of the following:** temperature controlled clothing; heated blankets; soft interfaces; **any other sensible answer**.
4. **Accept any two of the following:** hat; jacket; backpack; **any other sensible answer**.
5. **Accept any two of the following:** scents; drugs / chemicals; sensors.

Answers to Practice Questions
Page 52–53
1. **a)** staple.
    b) filament.

Answers

2. **a)–b) In any order:** animals; plants.
3. B and E.
4. **a)–d) In any order:** knitted; woven; felted; bonded.
5. Weft is knitted in horizontal rows and warp is knitted in vertical rows.
6. Jacquard – Creates a complex woven fabric.
    Plain – Creates an interlocking pattern.
    Satin – Creates a smooth, shiny fabric.
7. Regenerated; chemicals.

8. A and C.
9. True.
10. Needle felts – Sharp points are pushed through layers of fibres.
    Wool felts – The fibres are matted together using a solution.
    Bonded fabrics – Adhesive, solvent or stitching joins the fibres together.
11. B.
12. Microscopic particles with specific chemical and physical properties.
13. Microscopic structures that can conduct heat and electricity.

Modelling and Construction

Quick Test Answers
Page 57
1. **Accept any one of the following:** It allows you to test and evaluate design ideas; You can practice skills / techniques.
2. Screen / silk-screen printing.
3. A (metallic oxide or salt) fixative used with natural / vegetable dyes.
4. **Any of:** tie-dye; batik.
5. Digital printing.
Page 59
1. Soap and water.
2. Stitching through two layers of fabric with wadding in-between creates surface texture.
3. Spreadsheet software.
4. **In any order:** You can evaluate designs without using materials; it is quicker than modelling with fabric; you can experiment with different colours / scales without having to start again each time; **any other sensible answer**.
5. **Accept any two of the following:** pattern making; creating repeat patterns; presenting ideas; image mapping; modelling different colours / patterns / scales.
Page 61
1. They are graded and you cut around the outline for the size you require.
2. Pattern blocks come in standard sizes determined by the BSI.
3. To take apart.
4. A model / prototype textiles product made from cheap fabric.
5. **Accept any two of the following:** to test design ideas; to show what the finished product will look like; to help identify modifications that are needed; to estimate costs; to estimate how much fabric is required for the finished product; to evaluate the number of pattern pieces needed; to practise construction skills.

Page 63
1. Tacking.
2. Overlock with safety stitch.
3. Plain seam.
4. French seam.

Answers to Practice Questions
Page 64–65
1. C.
2. A, D and E.
3. Shisha – An ethnic type of embellishment using small mirrors.
    Shibori – A Japanese technique for manipulating fabrics using steam.
    Appliqué – Reinforced fabric shapes sewn onto a fabric background.
    Toile – A prototype garment made from cheap fabric.
4. **a)–b)** Onion; beetroot; **any other sensible answer**.
5. B.
6. **Accept any five of the following:** cross-stitch; herringbone stitch; satin stitch; French knots; chain stitch; any other hand embroidery stitch.
7. B.
8. **a)–b) Accept any two of the following:** saves times; saves money; can make modifications without having to start again; **any other sensible answer**.
9. C.
10. D.
11. A2; B4; C3; D1.
12. Tailor's tacking.
13. **a)** Double-stitched / Flat-felled seam.
    b) French seam.
    c) Overlocked seam.

Safety and Standards

Quick Test Answers
Page 69
1. **In any order:** design; manufacture; after manufacture.
2. **Accept any two of the following:** abrasion / wear and tear; elasticity / stretch; absorbency; crease recovery; insulation; flammability; **any other sensible answer**.
3. British Standards Institution (BSI)
4. **Accept any one of the following:** acetate; polyester; nylon; acrylic; polypropylene; elastane.
5. **Accept any one of the following:** components must be securely attached / not too small so the child cannot choke on them; materials must not melt or catch fire; dyes, paint and inks must not contain harmful substances / allergens; fastenings must be safe; **any other sensible answer**.

Page 71
1. **In any order:** following safety procedures / guidelines; wearing protective clothing.
2. **Accept any three of the following:** injuries to fingers and hands from needles / machinery; eye injuries; injuries from associated equipment, e.g. scissors.
3. **Accept any three of the following:** Keep work area clean and tidy; never use a machine with damaged covers; don't carry too many things at once; keep bags and coats out of the way; learn the correct way to lift; **any other sensible answer**.
4. Control of Substances Hazardous to Health.

Safety and Standards (Cont.)

Answers to Practice Questions
Page 72–73
1. A, D, E and G.
2. A4; B3; C1; D5; E2.
3. property; method; conditions; fair.
4. **a)** British Standards Institution (BSI).
   b) It has a Kitemark.
5. **a)** Tested for flammability / to make sure it won't melt or catch fire.
   b) Tested to make sure they are attached securely / are not too small (to cause a choke hazard).

6. A, B and D.
7. Nylon – Burns quickly, shrinks, melts and drips.
   Cotton – Smells like burning paper and turns into grey powder.
   Acetate – Burns quickly and smells like vinegar.
   Wool – Burns slowly and smells like burning hair.
8. **a)–d) Accept any sensible answer.** See p.71 of GCSE Textiles Technology Essentials Revision Guide for guidance.

Manufacturing

Page 75
1. True.
2. A range of acceptable measurements (for QC checks).
3. **Any two of:** the overall timeline of a project; the separate tasks that need completing; timings for the separate tasks; the sequence of tasks.
4. It changes it.
5. Feedback.

Page 79
1. **Accept any two of the following:** effective means of presentation; reduces time taken to produce products; improves communication; reduces repetitive work; decreases cost; increases efficiency; **any other sensible answer.**
2. **Accept any three of the following:** instant messaging; email; video conferencing; Internet; blogging; E-retail; interactive design; social networking sites; virtual imaging; **any other sensible answer.**
3. **Accept any two of the following:** graphics software; specialised textiles software; scanner; digital camera; graphics tablet; digital printer; PDM software; CAD systems; **any other sensible answer.**
4. Pre-production; production; post-production.

Page 81
1. **Accept any sensible answer, e.g.** tights, socks, vest top (simple, cheap products).
2. Work is passed along a production line in which each operator has a different task to perform.
3. **Accept any sensible answer, e.g.** swimwear, beach towels, winter coat (seasonal products).

4. Off-the-peg garments are produced in large quantities in standard sizes; bespoke products are custom made for the client.
5. **Accept any one of the following:** less space is required for storage; no surplus materials are ordered; **any other sensible answer.**

Answers to Practice Questions
Page 82–83
1. **a)** Computer Integrated Manufacture.
   b) Computer Aided Administration.
   c) Computer Aided Design.
   d) Computer Aided Manufacture.
2. Sales – EPOS and PDM software.
   Distribution – RFID Tagging.
   Manufacturing and production – Lay planning software and computerised cutting tables.
   Design – Graphics tablet.
3. **a)** C
   b) A
   c) C
4. **a)** Control systems; flow.
   b) Inputs
5. C and F.
6. B.
7. Gantt chart.
8. A4; B1; C2; D3.

Advertising and Marketing

Page 85
1. **Accept any two of the following:** posters; point-of-sale displays; swing tickets; packaging; information booklets / brochures; window / shop floor displays; **any other sensible answer.**
2. Trading (buying and selling) products over the Internet (or by other electronic means).
3. Primary packaging is the packaging that the product is displayed and marketed in; secondary packaging is used during distribution.
4. **Accept any one of the following:** reduce the layers of packaging; only use recyclable materials; use biodegradable materials; **any other sensible answer.**

5. **Accept any three of the following:** what the product is; the ethical values of the product; the target market; whether protection is needed; whether it needs to be transparent / have a window; whether the customer will need to try it on / test the product in-store; whether it needs to be easy to carry / lightweight; **any other sensible answer.**

Page 87
1. **In any order:** permanent; swing tag; gummed.
2. Permanent.
3. In descending order (the fibre with the highest content first).
4. Keep away from naked flames.
5. An act that makes it illegal to make false claims about products (e.g. in advertising materials).

Answers

Advertising and Marketing (Cont.)

Answers to Practice Questions
Page 88–89

1. **a) i)–iii) a)–c) Accept any three of the following:** TV; posters / bill boards; radio; cinema; magazines; newspapers; trade magazines / journals; specialist websites; logos on uniforms / lorries; **any other sensible answer**.

   b) i)–ii) Accept any three of the following: posters; POS material; swing tickets; stickers; packaging; information booklets; displays; **any other sensible answer**.

2. C.

3. **a)–c) Accept any three of the following:** shops; supermarkets; mail order catalogues; E-retailers; **any other sensible answers**.

4. **a)** Secondary.
   b) Primary.
   c) Secondary.
   d) Primary.

5. **a)** Fibre content should be given in descending order (the highest content fibre first) using chemical names.

   b) A
   c) A, C, D and G.

6. **a)** Machine wash at 40^0 Celsius.
   b) Dry clean.

7. The Textiles Products Regulations – The fibre content of a fabric must be stated on a label.
   The Trade Descriptions Act – A company must not make claims about their products that are not true.
   The Weights and Measures Act – It is illegal to sell products that weigh less than the amount stated on the label.
   The Sale of Goods Act – Products must match their description, be fit for purpose and of satisfactory quality.

8. **a)–b) In any order:** children's nightwear; upholstered furniture.

9. **Accept any one of the following:** organic; no animal testing; made from recycled material; all parts are recyclable; **any other sensible answer**.

Acknowledgements

P.6 ©iStockphoto.com/ Joachim Angeltun

P.6 ©iStockphoto.com/ Chris Hellyar

P.7 ©iStockphoto.com/ Joan Loitz

P.15 ©iStockphoto.com/ Umbar Shakir

P.20 ©iStockphoto.com/ Summer woodcock

P.23 FSC Logo, © 1996 Forest Stewardship Council, Asociación Civil

P.23 The EU Ecolabel, with kind permission of the European Commission (http://ec.europa.eu/ecolabel)

P.23 European Energy Label, with kind permission of the Energy Saving Trust (www.energysavingtrust.org.uk)

P.23 Confidence in Textiles' Oeko-Tex® Label, The International Oeko-Tex® Association (www.oeko-tex.com)

P.23 Fairtrade Mark, Fairtrade Foundation (www.fairtrade.org.uk)

P.26 Mood board, reproduced with kind permission of Amy Mallabar

P.27 Trendstop.com, with kind permission of Trendstop.com. Trendstop.com is dedicated to constantly providing fast, focused and accurate fashion forecasts and global trend information online

P.28 ©iStockphoto.com/ Helle Bro Clemmensen

P.28 ©iStockphoto.com

P.31 ©iStockphoto.com/ Matt Knannlein

P.32 ©iStockphoto.com/ Haze McElhenny

P.36 SEM of cotton fabric, Eye of Science / Science Photo Library

P.36 Coloured SEM of hollow viscose fibres, Science Photo Library

P.40 Forensic training (paper suits), Michael Donne / Science Photo Library

P.40 Eleksen fabric keyboard, courtesy of Peratech Limited

P.40 Ceramic fibre blanket, with kind permission of ceramicfiberonline.com

P.43 Spraying fabric, Colin Cuthbert / Science Photo Library

P.44 ©iStockphoto.com/ Camilla Wisbauer

P.44 ©iStockphoto.com

P.47 ©iStockphoto.com/ Greg Nicholas

P.48 ©iStockphoto.com/ Craig Veltri

P.49 AC0051 – Technical Tweed Cap – WLSS Tweed. © 2006 Musto Ltd, http://www.musto.co.uk. All rights reserved

P.50 Voltaic backpack, with kind permission of Voltaic Systems (www.voltaicsystems.com)

P.51 LifeShirt® Clinical, with kind permission of VivoMetrics, Inc (www.vivometrics.com)

P.54 ©iStockphoto.com/ Vera Bogaerts

P.54 ©iStockphoto.com

P.58 Herbaceous Border 1, with kind permission of Michelle Griffiths (www.shibori.co.uk). Michelle is a professional artist based in South Wales. Her work explores the natural rhythm of traditional Shibori techniques in order to create contemporary three dimensional sculptures. She is the World Shibori Network (www.shibori.org) representative for UK and Ireland

P.66 ©iStockphoto.com/ Christoph Kadur

P.68 BSI Kitemark and website, BSI Product Services (www.kitemark.com)

P.70 ©iStockphoto.com/ Lisa F. Young

P.77 Mark and 3D Runway Designer for PDS by OptiTex, with kind permission of OptiTex Ltd (www.optitex.com)

P.78 ©iStockphoto.com

P.85 ©iStockphoto.com/ Maurice van der Velden

P.86 ©iStockphoto.com/ Bart Claeys

P.86 ©iStockphoto.com/ Ciseren Korkut

P.86 ©iStockphoto.com/ Pawe Taajkowski

The following images are reproduced with the kind permission of Rapid Electronics Ltd., Severalls Lane, Colchester, Essex CO4 5JS. www.rapidonline.com

P.28 060554
P.48 064146
P.48 061052
P.48 061124
P.48 061142
P.57 061060

Controlled Assessment Guide

P.5 ©iStockphoto.com/ Natallia Bokach

P.6 ©iStockphoto.com/ Heidi Kalyani

P.14 ©iStockphoto.com/ Danny Hooks

All other images ©2009 Jupiterimages Corporation, and Lonsdale.

Index

Index